HKAC

10652365

A SAINT

FOR ALL REASONS

JUL 2010

A SAINT

FOR ALL REASONS

A pocket bible of 100 saints
for every situation

TIM MULDOON

Copyright © Ivy Press Limited 2010
All rights reserved.
Published in the United States of America by
QNY, an imprint of the Hammond World Atlas Corporation,
part of the Langenscheidt Publishing Group,
Long Island City, New York
www.langenscheidt.com

QNY and the QNY colophon are trademarks of the American Map Corporation

Catalog-in-Publication Data is available from the Library of Congress
ISBN-13: 978-0843-713817

Printed and bound in India

First edition
10 9 8 7 6 5 4 3 2 1

Ivy Press
This book was conceived, designed,
and produced by Ivy Press
210 High Street, Lewes
East Sussex BN7 2NS, UK
www.ivypress.co.uk

Creative Director Peter Bridgewater
Publisher Jason Hook
Editorial Director Tom Kitch
Art Director Wayne Blades
Senior Editor Polita Anderson
Designer Andrew Milne
Illustrations Sarah Young
Symbols Peters & Zabransky

CONTENTS

USING THE BOOK

 The collection of saints in this book covers many traditional patronages, but also offers new ideas about the ways in which saints' lives can inform our contemporary challenges. The saints represented here include those officially recognized in the Eastern and Western Churches (particularly the Orthodox, Catholic, Anglican, and Lutheran Churches) and those who have been designated "blessed" or "venerable" in those traditions.

This book offers you a saint for all reasons, a collection of blessed and venerable teachers to guide you in moments of crisis or indecision. It is a form of first-aid manual, if you will, offering the means to approach the appropriate saint for every material or spiritual crisis. The saints are grouped into chapters according to common themes, and can be sought by name or by subject using the indexes. If you find that you feel an affinity with a particular saint, we also provide a Web site from which you can download that saint's image to your computer or cell phone. Detailed instructions are included on the last page of the book.

SOLANUS CASEY

Housework

Solanus was the son of Irish immigrants, and born in Wisconsin in 1870. He had a variety of jobs in young adulthood—logger, hospital orderly, streetcar operator, and prison guard—before entering a diocesan seminary in his 21st year. Eventually he joined the Capuchin Franciscan order. He ministered for 20 years around New York City, before entering St. Bonaventure Monastery in Detroit. He spent another 20 years there, becoming known as "The Door-keeper." He was a much sought-after spiritual guide, even in this humble role, being willing to listen to anyone day or night.

....

RITUAL | PLACE A CRUCIFIX OVER THE FRONT DOOR OF YOUR HOME, AS A WAY OF REMINDING YOURSELF AND YOUR VISITORS THAT IT IS A SACRED PLACE. WHEN DOING HOUSEWORK, MAKE A SIMPLE SIGN OF THE CROSS TO RECALL THAT WHAT YOU ARE DOING IS THE HOLY WORK OF HOSPITALITY, MAKING YOUR HOME A PLACE WHERE PEOPLE PRACTICE WORKS OF LOVE. "PRACTICE HOSPITALITY UNGRUDGINGLY TOWARD ONE ANOTHER." (1 PETER 4:9)

....

PRAYER | *Lord, may the work that I do create a holy space for my family and all those who visit here. In loving each other, may we be doing the work of your kingdom.*

Home Decoration

 THIS GIFTED PAINTER and manuscript illustrator was a 15th-century woman born into a diplomat's family, who chose a life of poverty among the Poor Clares, the Franciscan order of women. She was a mystic and a visionary whose love of beauty expressed her spirituality. Her vision one Christmas eve of Mary and the Christ child may have inspired her to paint this same image in rich colors.

....

RITUAL | FIND A PLACE IN YOUR HOME TO HANG A BRANCH OR WREATH OF AN EVERGREEN TREE, AS A REMINDER TO CREATE BEAUTY IN THE HOME AS AN ECHO OF THE BEAUTY IN THE WORLD THAT GOD HAS CREATED.

....

PRAYER | *God, grant that this place where we live might remind us of the beauty of your presence in all creation.*

CATHERINE OF BOLOGNA

ZITA OF LUCCA

Homemakers

 FLORENTINE POET DANTE described the inhabitants of hell in his graphic epic poem *Inferno* in 1300, but a bright spot in his narrative is the city of Lucca, called "Santa Zita" after the humble housekeeper whom its residents admired. She was a servant all her life, but looked on her work as the way in which she could serve God. She often gave food to those who were even poorer than she, sometimes getting into trouble with the house's owners. Eventually they recognized her work and placed her in charge of the household.

....

RITUAL | DURING HOUSECLEANING, RECITE THE FOLLOWING PRAYER IN ORDER TO CONSECRATE YOUR WORK.

....

PRAYER | *God, bless my work today and grant that this home might be a place where peace will prevail and love will be abundant.*

Marriage

 Blessed Louis and Blessed Zélie (née Maria Azelia Guérin) are exceptional: both were lifelong lay people, the parents of nine children in late 19th-century France. Their youngest child was St. Thérèse of Lisieux (*see page 83*), who wrote of her parents, "The good God gave me a father and a mother who were more worthy of heaven than of earth." Both Louis and Zélie had at some time desired religious life, but eventually found each other and lived their married life as one consecrated to God. They considered living a Josephite (celibate) marriage, but through the counsel of a confessor were persuaded to have children as a way of living their vocation.

....

RITUAL | PRAY TOGETHER BEFORE LOVEMAKING.

....

PRAYER | *God, you made Adam and Eve to be a help and support to each other; and from these two the human race descended. You said, "It is not good for the man to be alone; let us make him a partner like himself." Now, Lord, you know that I take this spouse of mine not because of lust, but for a noble purpose. Call down your mercy on us, and allow us to live together to a happy old age.* (Tobit 8:5–7)

LOUIS & ZÉLIE MARTIN

11

JOSEPH

Adoption

 THE CARPENTER JOSEPH, from Nazareth, faced criticism and public scorn by marrying a woman who was already pregnant. The scriptures extolled marriages that produced children to build the kingdom of Israel; it must have been hard for him to adopt as his own son a child who did not share his bloodline. We know little about him from the gospels, but can assume that he raised Jesus to be a generous carpenter, just as he was.

. . . .

RITUAL | EVERY MOTHER'S DAY AND EVERY FATHER'S DAY DO SOMETHING ON BEHALF OF ADOPTIVE CHILDREN AND THEIR PARENTS: MAKE A DONATION TO AN ORPHANAGE; OFFER UP A PRAYER ON BEHALF OF THOSE FAMILIES WHO ARE YET TO BE UNITED; SEND A CARD TO FOSTER PARENTS IN YOUR COMMUNITY.

. . . .

PRAYER | *Joseph, you risked your reputation for the sake of your new wife and your adopted son. We ask for your prayers on behalf of children in need of parents, and of parents seeking a child. God, create in us generous hearts like that of Joseph, to make room in our lives for adoption and foster parenting.*

MONICA

Mothers

 OUR KNOWLEDGE of St. Monica comes from the autobiography of her son Augustine. She was a lifelong Christian, married to a Roman soldier who did not share her faith until his deathbed conversion. Augustine himself led a wild life, even as Monica prayed fervently that he would come to the faith. She sent him to St. Ambrose, who had helped form her own faith. Ambrose was a key figure in Augustine's conversion to Christianity, and later on Augustine wrote about how important his mother's prayers were in his life.

RITUAL | WRITE DOWN A PRAYER THAT IS SPECIFIC TO EACH OF YOUR CHILDREN, WHETHER YOUNG OR OLD, AT HOME OR AWAY FROM HOME. ASK GOD FOR THE SPECIFIC BLESSINGS THAT YOU HOPE FOR YOUR CHILD.

PRAYER | *Monica, you know the stress and hard work of loving a child, of hoping for your child's good even as he/she chooses a different way. Pray for me, and pray for my children, that they might listen carefully to the whisperings of the Holy Spirit moving them toward their truest joy.*

Fathers

 Louis, King of France for 44 years during the 13th century and also a member of the third order of Trinitarians, was the model of a fruitful life as a husband, a father of 11 children, and civil servant. He is invoked as a patron of large families, and is particularly regarded as a patron of fathers because of his ability to balance his many commitments.

RITUAL | AT NIGHT, MAKE A SIGN OF THE CROSS ON YOUR CHILDREN'S FOREHEADS AND BLESS THEM WITH THE PRAYER BELOW. IF THEY ARE AWAY FROM HOME, SAY THE PRAYER WHEN YOU GO TO SLEEP.

PRAYER | *God, bless my child and keep him or her in your care tonight and always. In the name of the Father, and of the Son, and of the Holy Spirit, Amen.*

LOUIS IX

EUGENE DE MAZENOD

Dysfunctional Families

 EUGENE'S GRANDMOTHER and aunt used to constantly meddle when he was young, reminding him that they were the source of money, while his parents fought constantly. Eugene moved several times due to the French Revolution, and got involved with an unruly group of friends. He tried unsuccessfully to reunite his parents after they divorced, which was uncommon in the 18th century. He later taught catechism and worked with prisoners. After a mystical experience of God's love, he sought ordination, and eventually founded the Oblates of Mary Immaculate.

. . . .

RITUAL | AT TIMES OF FAMILY DISCORD, ASK FOR EUGENE'S PRAYERS.

. . . .

PRAYER | *Eugene, you knew the stresses of a difficult family life. Pray for us now to discern more clearly how to love as Jesus did.*

Divorce

BORN OF HUMBLE PARENTS, Helena was an innkeeper who married a rising politician. After she gave birth to an only son, her husband acquired an important role in the Roman Empire and then divorced her in order to remarry for political connections. But when her son, Constantine, replaced his father, he honored Helena, striking coins in her image and renaming her birthplace Helenopolis. She used her influence to serve the faith and, ultimately, to make a pilgrimage to Jerusalem to find the true cross.

HELENA

RITUAL | ON THE FEAST DAY OF THE HOLY FAMILY (THE SUNDAY OF CHRISTMAS WEEK), SAY A PRAYER FOR THOSE WHO HAVE EXPERIENCED DIVORCE. CARRY A SMALL WOODEN CROSS.

PRAYER | *Helena, instead of bitterness, you carried with you a desire to share faith and hope with others. Pray that we who have been hurt in relationships may share your freedom to live generously.*

17

GAETANA STERNI

Stepparents

 AT THE AGE OF 15, Gaetana's own family was in financial dire straits when she married a widower named Liberale and became the stepmother of his three children. Sadly, Liberale died within just three years, and his family demanded to care for the children, misunderstanding the love that she showed them. Showing compassion and serenity, Gaetana helped the children to understand the situation before returning to the home of her mother. She stayed at home for seven years before entering into service at a hospice for beggars, where she lived for 36 years until her death in 1889.

RITUAL | WHEN YOU ENCOUNTER STORIES LIKE CINDERELLA OR SNOW WHITE, WITH EVIL STEPPARENTS, PRAY FOR THE MANY STEPPARENTS AND CHILDREN WHO HAVE FORGED LOVING AND HAPPY RELATIONSHIPS.

Brothers & Sisters

THESE TWINS GREW UP in the mountains to the northeast of Rome in the 6th century. Benedict left to study, and became critical of the corruption of secular society, entering a band of Christian ascetics. Over time his discipline gained him the enmity of his brothers, who tried to poison him. Benedict left them and began founding small monasteries, eventually writing his famous monastic *Rule*, which is still used today. Scholastica was a member of a religious community who would often visit her brother to engage in spiritual conversation. Gregory the Great later wrote in a story that, on one such occasion, she was so distressed at his decision to leave that she wept and prayed, and God answered her prayer with a torrential rainfall because her love was the greater of the two. At her death soon afterward, Benedict had her buried in his own tomb.

RITUAL | ON YOUR SIBLING'S BIRTHDAY, PLACE A DROP OF HOLY WATER ON A CARD AND PRAY THE FOLLOWING WORDS.

PRAYER | *God, thank you for the gift of my sister / brother. Bless her / him today, and let her / him know how much I love her / him, even when we disagree.*

BENEDICT & SCHOLASTICA

JOACHIM

Grandparents

 JOACHIM WAS A WEALTHY Galilean who gave regularly to the poor. Both he and his wife, Anne, were infertile until he went into the desert to fast for 40 days and then offer up a sacrifice. He and Anne both had visions that they would give birth to Mary. Joachim is not mentioned in the gospels, but he became venerated in early Church tradition for his role as the grandfather of Jesus.

RITUAL | MAKE SOME KIND OF OFFERING TO GOD ON YOUR GRANDCHILDREN'S BIRTHDAYS: PERHAPS A DONATION TO A LOCAL CHURCH OR TO A CHARITY THAT YOU WOULD LIKE TO SUPPORT.

PRAYER | *God, thank you for blessing our family with children and grandchildren. May they live to build your kingdom and thereby draw happiness, in the company of all of us who love them.*

Homeless

 BENEDICT WAS BORN into a middle-class family in 18th-century France. He was rejected by several religious orders and spent his life as a homeless person. He wandered the streets of cities, praying in cathedrals and begging for food, which he shared with his fellow homeless. Many healings were attributed to him soon after his death.

RITUAL | EVERY TIME YOU SHOP FOR FOOD, BUY AT LEAST ONE ITEM THAT WILL GO TO A LOCAL FOOD PANTRY OR SOUP KITCHEN.

PRAYER | *Grant that in our times of prosperity, our homes may be places where we can nourish our bodies, our minds, and our souls to serve you as generously as Benedict. And grant that in our times of need, the loss of a home may give us a new way to serve you.*

BENEDICT JOSEPH LABRE

DWYNWEN

Single Women

 DWYNWEN WAS a Welsh girl born in the 5th century, whose striking beauty captured the heart of a young man. Her own heart was set on religious life, however, so she prayed that he might be released from his infatuation. Yet she also prayed for all lovers, and because of that prayer her shrine at Llanddwyn (which is named after her) became a wishing well and pilgrimage site for young women over the centuries.

....

RITUAL | WHETHER YOU SEEK A FULFILLING SINGLE LIFE OR A FULFILLING MARRIED LIFE, PRAY ON DWYNWEN'S FEAST DAY (JANUARY 25) THAT GOD WILL LEAD YOU TO SERVE HIM WITH JOY.

....

PRAYER | *God, show me the way in which you are inviting me to pour out my life in love.*

Single Men

 THE RECENTLY BEATIFIED FOUNDER of the Society of St. Vincent de Paul was a young scholar at the time of the political disputes of mid-18th-century France. An intense worker, Frédéric studied law and literature, seeking to understand his vocation in life. At the age of 22, he penned a letter to a friend: "I sense within me a great void, which neither friendship nor study can fill. I do not know who will fill it: God, or a creature? If it is to be a creature, then I pray that it will be later, when I am worthy of her." It turned out to be later, when he married Amélie Soulacroix. He wrote to her: "I cannot offer you the conveniences of an amiable life of leisure... I give you the will of a man, an upright and honest will, the will to be good so as to make you happy." They married on June 23, and every month he would give his wife flowers on the 23rd.

RITUAL | CHOOSE AN ACT OF LOVE TO PERFORM ON THE 23RD DAY OF EACH MONTH.

PRAYER | *"Love never gives up. Love cares for others more than for self."* (1 Corinthians 13:4)

FRÉDÉRIC OZANAM

AUGUSTINE

Longing for Love

 THIS DOCTOR OF THE CHURCH wrote his most famous work, the autobiographical *Confessions*, at the end of the 4th century as a prayer of praise and thanksgiving to the God who rescued him from the lacerations of false desire he experienced in young adulthood. After many prayers by his mother, Monica *(see page 14)*, Augustine's intellectual and spiritual pilgrimage took him through various philosophies to embrace the gospel, and later in life he could write of his love for God: "You have created us for yourself, and our hearts are restless until they come to rest in you." *(Confessions Book 1)*

....

RITUAL | ON AUGUSTINE'S FEAST DAY, AUGUST 28, PRAY THAT GOD MIGHT HELP YOU TO DISCERN HOW TO LIVE WITH PASSION.

....

PRAYER | *God, show me how to love with complete abandon.*

Lovers

 THE VALENTINE'S DAY custom of sending love letters seems to arise from an ancient observation that mid-February was the time when birds would find mates. The feast of the 3rd-century martyr Valentine has now come to be synonymous with romantic love.

RITUAL | PROPOSE A TOAST TO LOVERS USING ONE CUP OF WATER AND ONE CUP OF WINE. THE IMAGE RECALLS JESUS' MIRACLE AT THE WEDDING IN CANA, AT WHICH HE CHANGED WATER INTO WINE SO THAT THE HAPPINESS OF THE GUESTS MIGHT NOT BE CUT SHORT.

PRAYER | *God, who created us in your image capable of great love, gladden the hearts of lovers, that they may delight in each other and, in their delight, know something of the joy for which you have created us.*

VALENTINE

ELIZABETH OF PORTUGAL

Wives

 THIS ELIZABETH, who was named after her great-aunt St. Elizabeth of Hungary, came from a royal family. Her father was King Pedro III of Aragon, and her great-grandfather was Emperor Frederick II. By the time she was a teenager, she was the married Queen of Portugal. Like her great-aunt, she was known for her service to the poor and sick. She was also known as a peacemaker, reconciling her son Affonso with her husband on one occasion when there was a threat of war. Late in her life she retired to a convent of Poor Clares, and even during that time she went out to prevent war between Affonso and his son-in-law. She is thus known as a patroness of wives and mothers, as well as of peacemakers.

....

RITUAL | AT MOMENTS WHEN YOU FEEL YOU ARE BEING PULLED IN DIFFERENT DIRECTIONS, RECALL THE WORDS OF JESUS IN THE BEATITUDES: "BLESSED ARE THE PEACEMAKERS."

....

PRAYER | *God, bless all the ways I try to love my family. Help me when I feel stretched; help me to know how to balance care for others with care for myself.*

Husbands

 FRANCIS WAS BORN of Spanish nobility, the paternal great-grandson of Pope Alexander VI and the maternal great-grandson of King Ferdinand II of Aragon. He married a Portuguese noble-woman, with whom he raised eight children. He served in public leadership positions, and was known for his faithfulness to his family and the Church. After his wife's death he joined the Jesuits and eventually became the Superior General, becoming known as its second founder, after Ignatius of Loyola. He is a model of love for one's family, love for one's fellow citizens, and love for the Church.

RITUAL | UPON RETURNING HOME EACH DAY, PRAY FOR BALANCE OF WORK AND FAMILY LIFE.

PRAYER | *God, bless all the ways I try to love and provide for my family.*

FRANCIS BORGIA

PATRICK

Love of Country

 THIS APOSTLE OF IRELAND was a 5th-century Roman Briton brought to Ireland as a slave at 14 years of age. After six years Patrick escaped, returning home and entering the religious life. He studied at different places in Europe and was eventually made a bishop. He had a vision that exhorted him to return to Ireland; Pope Celestine I sent him there to preach the gospel. He did this for 40 years, and the impressions he left were such that hundreds of years later his stories were circulated among the historians of Ireland. His name has since become synonymous with the national pride of many Irish around the world.

. . . .

RITUAL | ON MARCH 17, PRAY THE WORDS GIVEN BELOW, WHICH ARE TAKEN FROM AN 8TH-CENTURY HYMN ATTRIBUTED TO ST. PATRICK.

. . . .

PRAYER | *Christ be with me, Christ within me,*
Christ behind me, Christ before me,
Christ beside me, Christ to win me,
Christ to comfort and restore me,
Christ beneath me, Christ above me,
Christ in quiet, Christ in danger,
Christ in hearts of all that love me,
Christ in mouth of friend and stranger.

Loss of Parents

 EDITH WAS BORN of Jewish parents, but her father died when she was only one year old. She earned a doctorate in philosophy and later converted to Christianity. Later still she entered the Carmelite order as Teresa Benedicta of the Cross. Although she moved from Germany to the Netherlands to avoid Nazi persecution, she was arrested in 1942 and sent to the Auschwitz concentration camp where she died.

....

RITUAL | REMEMBER YOUR PARENT'S DEATH WITH EDITH'S WORDS BELOW.

....

PRAYER | *God, enkindle your love in me and then walk with me along the next stretch of road before me. I do not see very far ahead, but when I have arrived where the horizon now closes down, a new prospect will open before me, and I shall meet it with peace.* (St. Teresa Benedicta of the Cross)

EDITH STEIN

PAMMACHIUS

Widowers

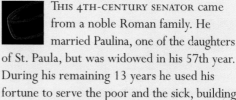 THIS 4TH-CENTURY SENATOR came from a noble Roman family. He married Paulina, one of the daughters of St. Paula, but was widowed in his 57th year. During his remaining 13 years he used his fortune to serve the poor and the sick, building a hospital with St. Fabiola. He built the church of St. John and St. Paul in Rome. He was also a friend of St. Jerome and St. Augustine. Jerome dedicated several commentaries on scripture to his old friend Pammachius, with whom he had studied rhetoric as a youth.

....

RITUAL | ON THE ANNIVERSARY OF YOUR WIFE'S DEATH, SEND A CONTRIBUTION IN HER NAME TO A CHURCH OR CHARITY THAT SERVES THE POOR OR SICK.

....

PRAYER | *God, you showed Pammachius ways to give himself in love after he lost his wife. Show me too how I might continue to give of myself to the world. Thank you for the gift that my wife was to me.*

Longing for a Child

 THE MOTHER of John the Baptist waited many years to have a child and was considered infertile until, at an advanced age, a son was promised to her by the Angel Gabriel. She was one of the first to know about Mary's great blessing as the Mother of God. Elizabeth waited patiently for the gospel story to unfold in her own life.

ELIZABETH

....

RITUAL | WHEN YOU HAVE YOUR PERIOD, SPEND SOME TIME IN SILENCE, MINDFUL OF THE PSALMIST'S WORDS "BE STILL AND KNOW THAT I AM GOD." BRING YOUR HOPE, FEAR, LAMENT, ANGER, AND DESPERATION BEFORE THE GOD WHO LOVES YOU MYSTERIOUSLY.

....

PRAYER | *Lord, you know my feelings because you know me better than I know myself* (Psalm 139). *Answer my prayer to love a child; show me how I might respond to this longing in my heart.*

ELIZABETH ANN SETON

Widows

 ELIZABETH WAS BORN into a wealthy family in 1774, and married a successful businessman at the age of 19. She bore five children, but before she was 30 her husband's business failed and he died. To support her children, she opened a school in Boston. She went on to found the Sisters of Charity, which still run schools today.

....

RITUAL | KEEP AN EMPTY WINE GLASS IN A DRESSER DRAWER, TO SYMBOLIZE THE LOSS OF THE JOY OF YOUR HUSBAND'S PRESENCE, BUT ALSO A READINESS FOR GOD TO REFILL THE GLASS WITH THE JOY OF NEW WAYS TO LIVE A LIFE OF SERVICE.

....

PRAYER | *Lord, your daughter Elizabeth Ann knew the sorrow of losing a husband. Strengthen me as you strengthened her, to find new ways to pour out my life in love for those around me.*

Love for Children

GIANNA WAS A PEDIATRICIAN who, in her younger years, was active in various ministries, including the St. Vincent de Paul Society. After her marriage to Pietro Molla in 1955, she found ways to balance her vocation as a doctor with that of wife and mother of three children. While pregnant with her fourth child, she developed complications; in the second month she had surgery to remove an ovarian cyst, pleading with the surgeon to save the child's life, and refusing to consider advice to have an abortion. The surgery was successful, but seven months later, after she gave birth to Gianna Emanuela, she died of complications resulting from the birth.

RITUAL | FIND A WAY TO HONOR YOUR CHILDREN ON THE ANNIVERSARY OF THEIR CONCEPTION, AS WELL AS THE ANNIVERSARY OF THEIR BIRTH.

GIANNA BERETTA MOLLA

33

Friendship

 A 12TH-CENTURY CISTERCIAN MONK who served as Abbot of Rievaulx Abbey in North Yorkshire, England for 20 years, Aelred wrote a remarkable treatise on friendship, offering the idea that "God is friendship." He was regarded as a saint during his lifetime.

RITUAL | PRAY FOR YOUR FRIENDS, AND BLESS THEM ON THEIR BIRTHDAYS.

PRAYER | *Sweet Lord, release wisdom from the seat of your greatness that it may be with us, toil with us, work with us, speak in us; may it, according to your good pleasure, direct our thoughts, words, and all our works and counsels, to the honor of your Name, the profit of the community, and our salvation; through our friend Jesus Christ, to whom with you and the Holy Spirit be honor and glory throughout all ages. Amen.* (Adapted from "St. Aelred's Pastoral Prayer" by L. Paul Woodrum)

AELRED OF RIEVAULX

Love of Animals

 THIS 14TH-CENTURY FRENCH nobleman was orphaned at 20, and gave away his money to the poor in order to live as a pilgrim. Along his travels he met plague victims, so he stayed to minister to them, effecting cures for which he became well known. Roch eventually succumbed to the plague himself, and went off to a forest to die. His patronage of animals, especially dogs, comes from a story of a dog finding him in the forest to bring him food until he recovered.

....

RITUAL | RECALL ROCH'S FEAST DAY ON AUGUST 16 BY SUPPORTING ANIMAL-CARE ORGANIZATIONS.

....

PRAYER | *Blessed are you, Lord, God of all creation, creator of all things big and small. Thank you for the gift of all your creatures. May we who care for them be faithful stewards, and may we learn to love more generously through our care for them.*

ROCH

Unemployed

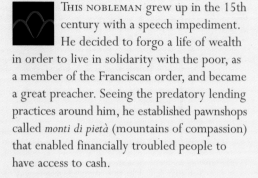 THIS NOBLEMAN grew up in the 15th century with a speech impediment. He decided to forgo a life of wealth in order to live in solidarity with the poor, as a member of the Franciscan order, and became a great preacher. Seeing the predatory lending practices around him, he established pawnshops called *monti di pietà* (mountains of compassion) that enabled financially troubled people to have access to cash.

....

RITUAL | AT THE BEGINNING OF EACH WORKDAY, GIVE THANKS TO GOD FOR THE ABILITY TO PAY THE BILLS. IN TIMES OF UNEMPLOYMENT, INVOKE THE NAME OF BLESSED BERNARDINO AND PRAY THAT GOD MIGHT LEAD YOU TO THE PERSON WHO WILL HIRE YOU NEXT.

....

PRAYER | *Lord, thank you for the gifts that enable me to do good work. Help me to find the place where I might use those gifts fully, to help build your kingdom of justice and freedom.*

....

OFFERING | Clear out all your unnecessary clothing, furniture, and household items and donate them to a local thrift store.

....

BERNARDINO OF FELTRE

Teachers

 JEAN STUDIED for the priesthood, but left to care for his brothers and sisters after his parents' death. Later, after finishing his studies, he founded the Christian Brothers order in 1680, dedicated to teaching children. He gave away his fortune to help the poor and endow his own work as a teacher. His order continues to teach children and young adults around the world.

. . . .

RITUAL | EVERY APRIL 7, OFFER A PRAYER AND A DONATION ON BEHALF OF UNDERPRIVILEGED STUDENTS.

. . . .

PRAYER | *St. Jean, help me to be as willing to teach young people as you were. Help me to share my faith and my knowledge with the children I encounter in my life. Bless all students with the love of caring teachers.*

JEAN BAPTISTE DE LA SALLE

Students

MARY MACKILLOP

 MARY WAS THE DAUGHTER of Scottish emigrants to Australia. She became a teacher and entered religious life, eventually founding the Sisters of St. Joseph of the Sacred Heart, Australia's first religious order, in 1866. She felt the call to establish schools for the poor, especially in remote areas, and worked to improve conditions for the Aboriginal people.

. . . .

RITUAL | SEND A CARD OR LETTER TO A TEACHER IN YOUR LIFE OR IN THE LIFE OF YOUR CHILD OR GRANDCHILD, THANKING HIM OR HER FOR THE GENEROUS GIFT OF SELF.

. . . .

PRAYER | *Jesus, you were called "Teacher," and know the liberation of education. Bless those who have taught me, and all teachers who give of themselves in love to educate children.*

Building

 THIS 14TH-CENTURY DOMINICAN was the son of an Anglo-Scottish nobleman and his Spanish wife. He earned his doctorate in theology and became a famous preacher throughout Europe and an adviser to Pope Benedict III and the King of Aragon. His patronage of builders comes from his reputation of having worked with great passion to build the Church.

RITUAL | ON APRIL 5, RECALL VINCENT FERRER AND PRAY BOTH FOR THOSE WHO BUILD FOR THE SAKE OF HUMAN SOCIETY AND COMFORT, AND FOR THOSE WHO BUILD UP THE CHURCH FOR THE SAKE OF CREATING A MORE JUST AND LOVING WORLD. "STRIVE TO EXCEL IN BUILDING UP THE CHURCH." (*1 CORINTHIANS 14:12*)

PRAYER | *Lord, bless those whose hands give shelter, and those whose actions give comfort.*

VINCENT FERRER

Military

 GEORGE WAS A TURKISH-BORN Roman soldier, and according to legend he slayed a dragon to save the daughter of the king. He then preached a sermon and converted those listening, exhorting them to be baptized and to take care of the poor. He is the patron of many different countries and cities, a role model of the soldier, whose task is to protect the innocent from harm. Of him, Edmund Spenser wrote these lines:

But on his breast a bloody Cross he bore,
The dear remembrance of his dying Lord,
For whose sweet sake that glorious badge we wore,
And dead (as living) ever he adored.

RITUAL | WHEN DRESSING IN MILITARY UNIFORM, ASK FOR THE BENEDICTION OF ST. GEORGE, PRAYING THAT YOUR STRENGTH AND COURAGE MIGHT BE USED FOR THE PROTECTION OF THE INNOCENT AND THE ESTABLISHMENT OF A JUST SOCIETY.

PRAYER | *Christ, give me the courage to fight with patience and humility against evil. Grant wisdom to my leaders, that they might never send us to do harm. Guide my actions, that I may discharge my duties with honor and be a servant to justice.*

GEORGE

THOMAS MORE

Law

 THE "MAN FOR ALL SEASONS," as Robert Bolt's play described Thomas More, was Lord Chancellor of England under Henry VIII. He was a devoted husband to Jane Colt, who bore him four children before her death. More then married a widow, Alice Middleton. He was a brilliant scholar and writer, author of the book that coined the term *utopia* ("no place"), about an idealized political philosophy. Devoted to the Church, More resigned the chancellorship when Henry sought to make himself the head of the Church in England. He was executed, a prisoner of conscience who described himself on the scaffold as "the king's good servant—but God's first."

....

RITUAL | ON A NATIONAL HOLIDAY, INVOKE THE NAME OF THOMAS MORE IN PRAYING FOR THE NATION.

....

PRAYER | *Lord, you created people for community. Grant that our country may serve your good by serving our common good. May we, like Thomas More, always seek to understand your will and act upon that understanding in the public arena.*

Business

 THE PATRON SAINT of business people, Homobonus was a 12th-century merchant renowned in his own time for his generosity toward the poor. He believed that God allowed his inheritance and fortune in business for the sake of helping others. Within two years of his death, Pope Innocent III canonized him, describing Homobonus (Latin for "good man") as a tree planted near the water, bearing fruit in our time (Psalm 1:3).

....

RITUAL | DESIGNATE A PART OF YOUR PROFITS TOWARD THE POOR.

....

PRAYER | *Lord, thank you for all the gifts that allow me to do profitable work. Grant me success, in order that the money I earn may benefit those in desperate need of help. St. Homobonus, pray for me.*

HOMOBONUS

43

FRANCIS DE SALES

Journalism

 THIS 16TH–17TH-CENTURY RESIDENT of the Savoy region in France was educated by the Jesuits and later earned doctorates in law and theology. Against the wishes of his family he entered religious life, and was eventually named Bishop of Geneva. He became renowned for his gentle, yet forceful explanation of Church doctrine. A gifted writer, he wrote hundreds of letters, many of which are still extant; and for his prolific writing he has become a patron of journalists and writers.

RITUAL | KEEP A SPIRITUAL JOURNAL THAT RECORDS DAILY OR WEEKLY REFLECTIONS ON THE QUESTION "WHERE IS GOD?"

PRAYER | *O love eternal, my soul needs and chooses you eternally! Ah, come Holy Spirit, and inflame our hearts with your love! To love —or to die! To die—and to love! To die to all other love in order to live in Jesus' love, so that we may not die eternally; but that we may live in your eternal love, O Savior of our souls, we eternally sing, "Live, Jesus! Jesus, I love! Live, Jesus, whom I love! Jesus, I love, Jesus who lives and reigns forever and ever." Amen.* (From Francis de Sales' *Treatise on the Love of God*)

Healthcare

As THE SON of an Italian military officer, Camillus also became a soldier, fighting in several conflicts in the late 16th century. He sustained foot and leg injuries that would trouble him all his life, and then worked in construction to pay off his debts; one of his jobs was for the Capuchin Friars, who converted him. He attended a hospital for incurables and eventually became its administrator. He founded the Congregation of the Servants of the Sick, and served the sick for the rest of his life.

....

RITUAL | AT THE BEGINNING OF EACH WORKDAY, PRAY TO SEE PATIENTS AS CAMILLUS DID, AS THE FACE OF CHRIST.

....

PRAYER | *Jesus, in your mercy you healed many sick. May my work too be an expression of your mercy today.*

CAMILLUS OF LELLIS

LOUISE DE MARILLAC

Social Service

 LOUISE WAS BORN in 1591 of an affluent Parisian family, but her mother died soon after childbirth. After a failed attempt to enter religious life, she found herself unmoored, but a spiritual director suggested that God had other plans for her. She married Antoine Le Gras and gave birth to a child, but soon Antoine got a chronic illness. Louise cared for both her husband and child for 13 years, wondering whether there might be anything else that life could offer her. She had the great blessing of spiritual direction from Francis de Sales and, after his death, from Vincent de Paul. After Antoine's death she maintained her role as a mother, but began to focus on her spiritual growth and charitable work. With Vincent she established the Daughters of Charity, a group of women dedicated to working in hospitals, orphanages, institutions for the elderly and mentally ill, prisons, schools, and on the battlefield.

RITUAL | AT THE END OF EACH BUSY DAY WITH YOUR FAMILY, PRAY FOR THE GREATER GOOD TO WHICH GOD IS INVITING YOU IN LOVE.

PRAYER | *God, help me understand how I might serve your people as Louise did.*

PAUL

Labor

 THE GREAT APOSTLE to the Gentiles was a tent maker by trade and made his living while laboring with the likes of Aquila (Acts 18:1–3). He esteemed good work, to the point of emphasizing that those who did not work should not eat (2 Thessalonians 3:10). He often used the image of labor to describe the unfolding of new life in Christ: "Each shall receive his wages according to his labor." (1 Corinthians 3:8)

RITUAL | WHEN YOU READ OR HEAR A TEXT OF ST. PAUL, MAKE A SIGN OF THE CROSS ON YOUR HANDS TO REMIND YOU OF HOW GOD HAS SANCTIFIED HUMAN WORK AS A PARTICIPATION IN THE WORK OF CREATION.

PRAYER | *Lord, you who send laborers into your vineyard, grant that the work I do may help to build your kingdom.*

Agriculture

 BORN TO POOR PARENTS in 11th-century Castile, outside Madrid, Isidore was a day laborer who was known to attend mass every day. One story tells that when his coworkers complained that he was avoiding work, an angel came and did his plowing for him. He was married to St. Maria Torribia, and they had one son who died young. They committed themselves to doing good works for the rest of their lives. After he died, many cures were attributed to Isidore.

· ·

RITUAL | EVERY TIME YOU EAT FRESH FRUIT OR VEGETABLES, LET IT BE A REMINDER OF THE GOOD WORK THAT FARM LABORERS DO EVERY DAY, OFTEN THANKLESSLY, RECALLING THE EXAMPLE OF ISIDORE.

· ·

PRAYER | *Lord, bless those whose hands bring forth the fruits of the Earth.*

ISIDORE THE FARMER

JOHN HENRY NEWMAN

College & University

 NEWMAN'S LIFE spanned nearly the entire 19th century. He was a fellow of Oriel College, Oxford, and a vicar of the University Church of St. Mary the Virgin, where he became well known for preaching university sermons. In seeking to revitalize the Church, he (along with Edward Pusey and John Keble) became a leading figure in the Oxford Movement, publishing many tracts on Christian life. His investigations into the early Church eventually led him to the Catholic Church in 1845. His writings anticipated much of the theological renewal of the Church in the 20th century.

RITUAL | WHEN UNIVERSITY CLASSES RESUME EACH YEAR, PRAY FOR THOSE WHO STUDY THERE TO BE GUIDED BY GOD'S WISDOM.

PRAYER | *I have my mission—I may never know it in this life, but I shall be told it in the next… Therefore, I will trust him… If I am in sickness, my sickness may serve him; in perplexity, my perplexity may serve him; if I am in sorrow, my sorrow may serve him… He does nothing in vain; he may prolong my life, he may shorten it, he knows what he is about.* (John Henry Newman)

Career

 THE PATRON OF VOCATIONS in the Church is also a model of listening to God to learn how to use one's talents. Alphonsus had a doctorate in law by the age of 16, played the harpsichord, and loved opera. He declined an arranged marriage, and entered religious life, founding the Redemptorist order in the early 1730s. He was made a bishop, and wrote and preached extensively. He vowed never to waste a day in his life, which lasted for 90 years.

. . . .

RITUAL | USE ALPHONSUS'S PRAYER BELOW WHEN CONSIDERING A LIFE DECISION. PRAY IT EVERY DAY UNTIL YOU KNOW WHAT TO DO.

. . . .

PRAYER | *Lord, take possession of us; we give our whole will to you; make us understand what it is that you desire of us, and we will perform it.* (St. Alphonsus Maria of Liguori)

ALPHONSUS OF LIGUORI

ANTHONY OF PADUA

Travelers

 THE EVANGELICAL DOCTOR is the patron saint of travelers, because his preaching was in such high demand that he traveled all over Italy and France. Anthony became one of the most beloved of saints after his death in 1231.

. . . .

RITUAL | THE PRAYER BELOW USES AN IMAGE OF TRAVEL AS A METAPHOR FOR THE JOURNEY OF LIFE, THE VOCATIONAL JOURNEY. RECITE THE PRAYER AT SIGNIFICANT MOMENTS IN THE LIVES OF THOSE YOU LOVE.

. . . .

PRAYER | *St. Anthony of Padua, you endured discouragement in your life before finding your calling. Help us to find patience in our own lives, and to trust God to lead us where we need to go. You preached by example; help us show others through example the truth of our faith. Amen.*

Pilgrimage

 THE MAGI FROM THE EAST described in Matthew's gospel are unnumbered and unnamed, but by the 8th century they had come to be known as Melchior, Caspar, and Balthasar. They have become part of the imaginative recollection of the Christmas story because of what they represent: a long journey to come into firsthand contact with the infant Jesus, to behold with their own eyes the newborn king of Israel and offer him homage, with lavish gifts of gold, frankincense, and myrrh.

....

RITUAL | MAKE A PILGRIMAGE TO AN IMPORTANT SITE, PERHAPS A HISTORICAL CHURCH OR A SHRINE. BRING WITH YOU AN OFFERING, EITHER FOR THE MAINTENANCE OF THE SITE OR FOR THE POOR OR SICK. CONSIDER THIS PILGRIMAGE A REFLECTION OF YOUR LONGER PILGRIMAGE TOWARD GOD.

....

PRAYER | *God, the hope of the Magi to see Jesus reflects our own hopes to see you face-to-face. May our own pilgrimage through life afford us the opportunity to see Jesus in the flesh.*

MELCHIOR, CASPAR, BALTHASAR

JOHN THE BAPTIST

Highways

 THE KINSMAN OF JESUS, and the son of Elizabeth, John lived as the prophet Isaiah had written: "In the wilderness prepare the way of the Lord, make straight in the desert a highway for our God." (Isaiah 40:3) He reminds us that making a highway is a metaphor for opening our lives to more perfectly imitate the Lord.

. . . .

RITUAL | USE THE TIME THAT YOU SPEND ON THE HIGHWAY TO MEDITATE ON THE STATE OF YOUR READINESS TO PREPARE A PLACE FOR GOD IN YOUR LIFE.

. . . .

PRAYER | *God, you sent your servant John to prepare a way for the coming of Christ. Help me to clear away whatever is in my life that keeps me from receiving your grace, and be ready to greet you with joy.*

Migrants

 FRANCES FOUNDED the Missionary Sisters of the Sacred Heart to care for poor children. Pope Leo XIII sent her to mission territory in the United States in 1889 to look after immigrants, especially those from Italy. She later became a U.S. citizen and was the first such to be declared a saint.

....

RITUAL | CHOOSE A NATIONAL FEAST DAY, AND TRAVEL TO A COMMUNITY OR A CONGREGATION THAT SERVES THE NEEDS OF IMMIGRANTS. WORSHIP IN A DIFFERENT LANGUAGE; HAVE A CONVERSATION WITH SOMEONE WHO SPEAKS A DIFFERENT FIRST LANGUAGE THAN YOU.

....

PRAYER | *Frances, you know what it is like to be an immigrant to a strange new land. Help those who are struggling to make a new home; help me to be a friendly face to those far from the land of their birth.*

FRANCES XAVIER CABRINI

MARTHA

Hotels

 MARTHA OF BETHANY, sister of Mary and Lazarus, appears three times in the gospels as a friend of Jesus. Luke's story of Jesus at their home describes Martha as the one who was busy about the house, providing hospitality for him while her sister stayed simply to listen to him. John describes her again as serving at a dinner for Jesus, six days before his death. Martha's gift to Jesus was her hospitality.

....

RITUAL | BLESS THE ENTRANCE OF A HOTEL WHERE YOU ARE STAYING BY PRAYING THE WORDS GIVEN BELOW.

....

PRAYER | *Father, you blessed the hands of Martha to serve Jesus by providing hospitality for him. Bless those whose hands have welcomed me here and have given me a place of rest.*

Automobile Drivers

THIS 3RD-CENTURY MARTYR is well known for his name, which in Greek means "Christ-bearer." The legend of Christopher, who is also known as Offero, is that he sought out a holy hermit who was living near a dangerous river. Christopher helped people to cross the river safely, including a small child, who later revealed himself to be the Christ child.

....

RITUAL | EVERY TIME YOU SIT BEHIND THE WHEEL OF AN AUTOMOBILE, TOUCH YOUR SHOULDER IN MEMORY OF CHRISTOPHER.

....

PRAYER | *God, you who have created all people in the image of your Son, grant that all those who are in my care as a driver be kept safe from harm. May I grant your children safe passage, just as Christopher granted safe passage to your Son.*

CHRISTOPHER

FRANCIS XAVIER

Travel to Foreign Lands

 A 16TH-CENTURY NOBLEMAN from the castle of Javier (Xavier) in the north of Spain, Francisco de Jaso y Azpilicueta was a member of the original group of seven companions who formed the Society of Jesus. Francis left on a mission to preach in Asia, where his preaching converted many thousands, partiularly in Goa, India; the East Indies; and Japan. He had hoped to make it to China, but died off its coast.

RITUAL | WHEN YOU CROSS THE BORDER OF YOUR HOME COUNTRY, MAKE A SIGN OF THE CROSS TO GIVE THANKS FOR THE GIFTS OF DIFFERENT LANDS, AND TO PRAY FOR GREATER UNITY.

PRAYER | *Lord, you sent Francis to spread the gospel of peace and truth. Help us to grow in understanding, and to work to build a world rooted in your love.*

Weather

 THIS 9TH-CENTURY BISHOP of Winchester was chaplain to the West Saxon king Egbert. Swithun was well regarded after his death. His patronage of the weather derives from a story about his grave site being moved indoors to a shrine in the cathedral. It rained for 40 days, giving rise to the popular belief that St. Swithun's day was a predictor of the weather:

> St. Swithun's day, if thou dost rain,
> For 40 days it will remain;
> Saint Swithun's day, if thou be fair,
> For 40 days 'twill rain nae mair.

SWITHUN

....

RITUAL | GIVE THANKS TO GOD FOR THE RAIN.

....

PRAYER | *He covers the heavens with clouds,*
he prepares rain for the Earth,
he makes grass grow upon the hills.
(Psalm 147:7–8)

Sea Travel

BORN IN 484 near present-day Tralee in County Kerry, Ireland, Brendan was a monk who established several monasteries. He studied under St. Ita and St. Erc, and was a friend of Saints Enda, Brigid, Columba, and Brendan of Birr. By the 11th century, a collection of stories known as *The Voyage of St. Brendan* was well known, describing a seven-year pilgrimage to find a paradise on Earth in the company of fellow monks. In one depiction the monks' boat rows heavenward, a symbol of our earthly pilgrimage.

RITUAL | PRAY FOR A SAFE VOYAGE, CONSIDERING THE IMAGE OF BRENDAN AS A METAPHOR FOR THE CHURCH AS A LATTER-DAY NOAH'S ARK.

PRAYER | *Let him pray that we may be saved*
As we sail upon this sea.
Let him quickly aid the fallen
Oppressed with burdensome sin.
(Hymn to Saint Brendan, by
Guido of Ivrea, 11th century;
English translation from the
Latin by Karen Rae Keck, 1994)

BRENDAN THE NAVIGATOR

Air Travel

 THE MOST COLORFUL of patron saints may be the saint for air travel, for Joseph was known for levitating in the air. He was born in 1603 after his father died, leaving his mother impoverished. Joseph was a poor student who was rejected by the Conventual Franciscans, but he was eventually admitted as an Oblate by the Capuchins at Cupertino. He was regularly given to ecstatic visions, and for 35 years was ordered to stay out of public view.

....

RITUAL | UPON EMBARKING ON AN AIRPLANE, PRAY FOR THE PILOTS.

....

PRAYER | *Lord, thank you for the ability to travel quickly by air. Bless those who are flying today. Give them good judgment and help them to arrive safely.*

JOSEPH OF CUPERTINO

BERNARD OF MONTJOUX

Mountains

BERNARD WAS A 10TH-CENTURY priest of Aosta, Italy. He is most well known for the two monasteries and hospices that he built in the Alps, along passes more than 7,000 feet (2,130m) high through which pilgrims to Rome often traveled. It was in these monasteries that we see the earliest records of the dogs that would be sent to aid travelers. In 1923 Pope Pius XI named Bernard the patron of skiers and mountain climbers.

RITUAL | WHEN ON A SNOWY MOUNTAINTOP, MAKE A CROSS IN THE SNOW AS A MEMORIAL TO THOSE WHO HAVE DIED.

PRAYER | *Praise to you, Lord God, for the beauty of those places where the earth rises to meet the sky. Thank you for the example of St. Bernard, and for all those who aid travelers in trouble.*

Rivers

 IN POPULAR MEDIEVAL LEGEND, Julian received a prophecy that he would kill his parents, so he moved far away. When they found him and came to visit, his wife insisted that his parents stay in their bedroom. Julian duly killed them, thinking they were his wife and another man. He later built a hospice beside a river. He rowed travelers across the river for free, and helped many pilgrims. One was a leper, to whom Julian gave his own bed. The leper was revealed to be an angel, saying that Christ had accepted Julian's penance.

....

RITUAL | UPON CROSSING A RIVER, GIVE THANKS FOR THOSE WHOSE LIVES AND WORK OVERCOME SEPARATION BETWEEN PEOPLE.

....

PRAYER | *Lord, thank you for bridge builders.*

JULIAN THE HOSPITALLER

ANTHONY OF EGYPT

Deserts

 St. Athanasius wrote a biography of Anthony, who is considered the father of monasticism. He was born in the mid-3rd century in Egypt, and at 20 he embarked upon an ascetic life, eventually moving into the desert to practice spiritual exercises alone. Yet many disciples followed him there, begging him to teach them. Anthony established two monasteries—an innovation that brought together spiritual ascetics for the sake of helping each other to achieve Christian perfection. He lived almost his entire life in the desert, plumbing the depths of the spiritual life, and was a great influence on later monastics such as St. Benedict.

RITUAL | CONSIDER THE FIERCE LANDSCAPE OF THE DESERT, THE PLACE WHERE CHRIST WAS TEMPTED BY THE DEVIL AND THE PLACE WHERE HE WITHDREW TO PRAY. UPON SEEING THE DESERT, DRAW A CROSS IN THE SAND.

PRAYER | *Lord, you sent Anthony into the desert to be free of distraction to come to know you. May we, too, come to know you even amid the business of life.*

Forests

HUBERT'S EXPERIENCE of conversion took place in a forest. A young and wealthy courtier in the 8th century, Hubert loved hunting, and on one occasion he saw a vision of the cross between the antlers of a deer. A voice told him to reform his ways, and he was greatly moved. After the death of his wife, he renounced his wealth and entered the priesthood, eventually being named the first Bishop of Liège. He was greatly revered in the Middle Ages, and several military orders were named after him.

....

RITUAL | PAUSE FOR A MINUTE UPON ENTERING ONE OF NATURE'S CATHEDRALS, AND GIVE THANKS TO THE GOD WHO CREATED IT.

....

PRAYER | *Lord, you made the forests the lungs of the Earth. Help us to preserve them, that their beauty might praise you.*

HUBERT OF LIÈGE

VERONICA

Photography

THE PIOUS LEGENDS about Veronica surfaced as early as the 4th century, though they are not mentioned in the gospel. By the early Middle Ages she was described as the one who wiped Jesus' face on his way to Calvary, so that the true image (*vera icon*, which became "Veronica") of his face was left on the cloth.

RITUAL | IF YOU HAVE A MEMENTO LIKE A PHOTOGRAPH THAT BRINGS TO MIND AN IMPORTANT PERSON IN YOUR LIFE, USE THAT ITEM TO ASK A QUESTION: HOW MIGHT A MEMENTO OF JESUS' LIFE AFFECT YOUR FAITH?

PRAYER | *Jesus, at times you seem distant. Help my unbelief by assisting me to see you in the images of the people I love from day to day. Let me always look for you in the newness of each day, and not lose sight of you by looking for you only in the past.*

Telephone

 IT DOES NOT TAKE A VAST LEAP of the imagination to see the connection between God's messenger (Greek *angelos*) and his patronage of the telephone. Gabriel (Hebrew for "God has shown himself mighty") features in the Book of Daniel and also in Luke's gospel, where he appears to Zechariah to announce the birth of John the Baptist. He is also the messenger of Mary to announce the coming of the Christ child. It is the scene of this latter Annunciation that is most frequently depicted in art.

. . . .

RITUAL | ON THE FEAST OF THE ANNUNCIATION (MARCH 25) CALL SOMEONE YOU LOVE JUST TO EXPRESS HOW MUCH HE OR SHE MEANS TO YOU.

. . . .

PRAYER | *Lord, you speak to us in many ways. May our words of love be your voice of comfort to the world.*

GABRIEL THE ARCHANGEL

CLARE OF ASSISI

Television

 CLARE WAS BORN of a noble family in Assisi in 1194, and expressed to her friend Francis her desire to enter religious life. She established the Poor Ladies (now known as the Poor Clares) and followed the Franciscans all over Europe, setting up convents. Eventually her mother and sisters joined the order. Clare's patronage of television is based on the time when she was near death and unable to attend mass, and the image of the celebration appeared on the wall of her cell. The story may have developed in part because of her name, which means "bright" and "clear."

. . . .

RITUAL | PAUSE FOR A MOMENT TO UTTER A PRAYER WHEN YOU TURN ON THE TELEVISION.

. . . .

PRAYER | *Lord, grant that my immediate vision never gets in the way of my desire to see you face-to-face.*

Environment

 KATERI WAS BORN in the 17th century to a Mohawk father and a Christian Algonquin mother, both of whom died during a smallpox epidemic. A Jesuit missionary baptized her in 1676 after her conversion, alienating her from her relatives. Tekakwitha (Mohawk for "she moves things") escaped to the Native American village of Kahnawake, Quebec, where she became known for her piety. Her example has moved many to learn about Native American spirituality, and its respect for the natural world as sacred space.

....

RITUAL | ON KATERI'S FEAST DAY (JULY 14), FAST FROM TECHNOLOGY BY "UNPLUGGING." SPEND TIME REVERENCING GOD'S CREATION.

....

PRAYER | *Lord, you have revealed yourself in the book of nature to those willing to behold. Help us to become beholders.*

KATERI TEKAKWITHA

GIUSEPPE MOSCATI

Medicine

 BORN IN 1880 in Benevento, Italy, Giuseppe was the first contemporary medical doctor to be declared a saint. He worked in a hospital for incurables in Naples, helped prepare for and respond to the eruption of Mount Vesuvius in 1906, and also worked amid a cholera epidemic in 1911. This distinguished physician, who directed several hospitals, believed that "One must attend first to the salvation of the soul and only then to that of the body." He often refused payment, especially from the poor and clergy, and helped many to regain their faith and religious practice.

. . . .

RITUAL | MAKE A DONATION ON BEHALF OF THE UNINSURED WHEN YOU RECEIVE HEALTH CARE.

. . . .

PRAYER | *Thank you, God, for the healing hands of those in the medical profession. May they serve the good of the bodies you have created.*

Internet

ISIDORE BEGAN LIFE as a poor student, but eventually succeeded his brother as Bishop of Seville and became a doctor of the Church. He worked to overcome the ethnic and racial differences among the various peoples of 7th-century Spain. His voluminous writings, including an encyclopedia, led the Council of Toledo to regard him as the most learned man of his age.

. . . .

RITUAL | EVERY TIME YOU USE THE INTERNET, WHISPER THE NAME OF ISIDORE AS A REMINDER OF HOW KNOWLEDGE CAN SERVE TO UNITE PEOPLE WHEN THEY ARE WEDDED TO LOVE AND JUSTICE.

. . . .

PRAYER | *Lord, your servant Isidore sought to bring his learning to the service of uniting people across racial and ethnic lines. Grant that I might use my knowledge for the sake of advancing your kingdom of mercy, your civilization of love.*

ISIDORE OF SEVILLE

71

ERASMUS

Electricity

St. Erasmus of Formia, also known as St. Elmo, was a patron of sailors, who during their voyages would often see the electrical discharge that bears the saint's name. Erasmus was a 3rd-century martyr, one of the Fourteen Holy Helpers called upon in medieval Europe as intercessors. One of the stories told about him took place during the persecutions of Diocletian: Erasmus was thrown into a pit of snakes, and lightning came down and electrocuted everyone around except him.

....

RITUAL | WHEN YOU SEE A LIGHTNING STORM, PRAY FOR SAILORS AND GIVE THANKS FOR PEOPLE WHO USE THEIR KNOWLEDGE TO HARVEST ELECTRICAL POWER FOR THE BENEFIT OF HUMANKIND.

....

PRAYER | *Lord, thank you for the energy that lights our world, and for the human ingenuity that puts it to the service of people.*

Economics

 FRANCESCO BERNARDONE was the son of a wealthy 12th-century merchant. He was a wild youth, fighting in frequent conflicts between rival cities Assisi and Perugia at the time. After his conversion, he took literally the gospel exhortation to leave everything and follow Jesus. When asked whether he was getting married, he said that his bride was fairer than any other, referring to "lady poverty." He founded the Order of Friars Minor, commonly known as the Franciscans, based upon a life of poverty.

PRAYER | *Lord, make me an instrument*
of your peace.
Where there is hatred, let me sow love;
where there is injury, pardon;
where there is doubt, faith;
where there is despair, hope;
where there is darkness, light;
and where there is sadness, joy.
Divine Master, grant that I may not so
much seek to be consoled as to console;
to be understood as to understand;
to be loved as to love.
For it is in giving that we receive;
it is in pardoning that we are pardoned;
and it is in dying that we are born to
eternal life. (St. Francis)

FRANCIS OF ASSISI

73

ALBERT THE GREAT

Science

 ALBERT OF COLOGNE was a 13th-century Dominican friar whose writings spanned the fields of botany, biology, chemistry, anthropology, philosophy, theology, and other subjects. Among his students was Thomas Aquinas, who like Albert drew from the basic philosophical methods of Aristotle, of observation of the natural world and enquiry into the causes of things. Albert was considered a great intellect in his time, composing some 38 volumes of writings. He was a Dominican provincial, as well as Bishop of Regensburg for three years. Among his scientific work was the discovery of arsenic.

. . . .

RITUAL | AS ALBERT'S SCIENTIFIC WORK BEGAN WITH A SENSE OF WONDER AT THE WORLD GOD HAD MADE, TAKE TIME TO READ ABOUT CONTEMPORARY SCIENCE AND TO WONDER AT THE WORLD.

. . . .

PRAYER | *God, thank you for both the awesome world we live in and for our ability to understand it through questioning and learning. Bless those whose work helps us understand the world and who use its elements to serve your creation.*

Communications

 BERNARDINO'S PATRONAGE of communications arose because of his remarkable ability to preach and gain converts. He was a 15th-century Franciscan, an itinerant preacher so committed to his vocation that he rejected three offers to become a bishop. He was also a peacemaker, who sought to balance the demands of Christian life against the codes of honor that divided feuding clans in the Italian cities where he preached. Among his allies were many women, who comprised the majority of his audiences.

....

RITUAL | FIND A WAY TO EXPRESS YOUR FAITH TO SOMEONE, EITHER IN WRITING OR IN SPEECH.

....

PRAYER | *Lord, you gave Bernardino the gift of speaking in order to preach your kingdom. Grant that we too might, through our lives and our communication, preach the gospel.*

BERNARDINO OF SIENA

75

FRA ANGELICO

Arts

 BROTHER GIOVANNI OF FIESOLE was born in 1395 with the name Guido di Pietro. He was already a painter when he joined the Dominican order, and he continued to paint religious themes all his life, adorning altarpieces, convents, and chapel walls. Pope Eugenius IV summoned him to Rome to paint the walls of a chapel at the Vatican. He was offered a bishopric, which he refused in order to keep painting. By the 16th century he was already known as Fra "Angelico."

....

RITUAL | PRAY BY USING A WORK OF ART THAT INSPIRES YOU.

....

PRAYER | *Thank you, Lord, for the gifts that you give to artists, to inspire us with beauty and to challenge us with hidden truth.*

Music

 POPE FROM 590 TO 603, Gregory was the first pope to come from the monastic tradition, having spent many years as a Benedictine and having founded several monasteries. Upon seeing English children being sold in the Roman forum, he became a missionary to England. He later sent St. Augustine of Canterbury and a company of monks to serve there. His patronage of music arises from his collection of many plainsong chants and melodies, now known as Gregorian chants. He is a doctor of the Church in the West, while in the East he is known as Gregory the Dialogist, after his *Dialogues,* one of many of his writings that are still extant.

....

RITUAL | VISIT A MONASTERY OR CONVENT AND PRAY THE LITURGY OF THE HOURS WITH MUSIC INSPIRED BY GREGORY'S WORK.

....

PRAYER | *Lord, our ancestors in faith taught us to praise you with music. Grant that those who produce music today might also praise you, and that our song might move us to ever greater faith, hope, and love.*

GREGORY THE GREAT

JOSEPHINE BAKHITA

Globalization

THIS DAUGHTER OF SUDAN was canonized by Pope John Paul II: "In our time, in which the unbridled race for power, money, and pleasure is the cause of so much distrust, violence, and loneliness, Sister Bakhita has been given to us once more by the Lord as a universal sister, so that she can reveal to us the secret of true happiness…" Josephine was born of a wealthy family in the Darfur region in 1868, but was captured by slave traders and sold many times. In 1883 an Italian diplomat bought her; she went with him to Italy and served as a nanny in the house of his friend Augusto Michieli. After she and the Michielis's daughter were left in the care of the Canossian Sisters, Josephine came to know God as a new, loving master: "I am definitively loved and whatever happens to me—I am awaited by this Love. And so my life is good." She remained with the Sisters for nearly 50 years and was beloved by all who met her.

....

RITUAL | PRAY FOR EXPLOITED PEOPLE IN THE WORLD USING THE WORDS GIVEN BELOW.

....

BLESSING | *Barikiwa mpaka ushangae* (Swahili for "Be blessed until you are amazed!")

MARTÍN DE PORRES

Social Justice

 THE FIRST BLACK SAINT from the Americas was the illegitimate son of a Spanish nobleman and a freed slave. His childhood was impoverished; his mother could not afford school, so she apprenticed him to a barber-surgeon to learn medicine. Later he served in a Dominican priory in Lima, and at the age of 24 his superiors dropped the stipulation against admitting blacks to the order. Martín worked on behalf of the poor, the sick, the marginalized, and the homeless of the city.

....

RITUAL | ON MARTÍN'S FEAST DAY, NOVEMBER 3, PLAN SOME SOCIAL WORK: A DAY OF SERVICE IN AN ORPHANAGE OR SOUP KITCHEN, OR A LONGER-TERM COMMITMENT OF REGULAR VOLUNTEERING.

....

PRAYER | *Lord, you call us to heaven, yet ask us to work in your vineyard on earth. Grant that we may do so with generous and loving hearts.*

Literature

 Good King Alfred was once claimed by University College, Oxford, as its founder. While scholarship has shown that claim to be dubious, what is clear is that this 9th-century King of the Anglo-Saxons came from Oxfordshire and was a man of great learning who, after repelling the Vikings, strove to advance scholarship and the rule of law in the kingdom, for the sake of his people's development. He himself was a great scholar, translating Boethius' *Consolation of Philosophy* into Old English from Latin.

....

RITUAL | UPON OPENING A BOOK, BEND THE CORNER OF A PAGE AS A REMINDER TO GIVE THANKS TO GOD FOR CREATIVITY AND LEARNING.

....

PRAYER | *Lord, you gave us words to help us understand your Word. Bless our language; may we use it always to praise you.*

ALFRED THE GREAT

Chronic Pain

 LYDWINA WAS BORN in late 14th-century Holland to a poor nobleman and his commoner wife. Devoted to Our Lady of Schiedam at a young age, she was injured in an ice-skating accident and developed complications. She became paralyzed and suffered for decades, developing a great devotion to the Eucharist and offering her sufferings to God. She was blind for the last seven years of her life. She was honored for centuries after her death, and was finally canonized in 1890.

RITUAL | OFFER YOUR PAIN TO GOD BY MEDITATING ON THE TEXT BELOW.

PRAYER | *Beloved, let those who suffer according to God's will do right and entrust their souls to a faithful Creator.* (1 Peter 4:19)

LYDWINA OF SCHIEDAM

Sick People

 FRANÇOISE-MARIE THÉRÈSE MARTIN, the youngest doctor of the Church, died at 24 of tuberculosis. Just before her 14th birthday she had a vision of the child Jesus and longed to enter religious life, but was refused because of her age. After meeting Pope Leo XIII she entered the Carmelites at the age of 15 with the name Thérèse of the Infant Jesus and the Holy Face, and made her final vows at 17. By the age of 20 she was Novice Mistress. Her superiors ordered her to write her memoirs, which later became known as *Story of a Soul,* and showed uncommon wisdom.

....

RITUAL | WHEN YOU ARE SICK, PIN THIS PRAYER ABOVE YOUR HEART, IMITATING THÉRÈSE'S OWN HABIT. ASK GOD THAT YOU MIGHT PRAISE HIM EVEN IN YOUR SICKNESS.

....

PRAYER | *Make me resemble you, Jesus!*

THÉRÈSE OF LISIEUX

KSENYA BLAZHENNAYA

Family Problems

 KSENYA BLAZHENNAYA, also known as Xenia of Petersburg, was born in the early 18th century and later married Colonel Andrei Feodorovich Petrov, who died when Ksenya was just 26. In her remaining 45 years many people considered her a fool: she took her husband's name and his clothes, and gave away all her worldly goods. Her family went to court to try to stop her charity, but the judge ruled in Ksenya's favor. She refused the help of her family, dedicating herself instead to work among the poor of St. Petersburg. At night she moved bricks to help the construction of the church in the Smolensk cemetery, where she was eventually buried.

....

RITUAL | GIVE AWAY SOMETHING VALUABLE; MAKE A GIFT TO THE POOR THAT OTHERS MIGHT CONSIDER FOOLISH.

....

PRAYER | *Having renounced the vanity of the earthly world, thou didst take up the cross of a homeless life of wandering; thou didst not fear grief, privation, nor the mockery of men, and didst know the love of Christ. Now taking sweet delight of this love in heaven, O Xenia, the blessed and divinely wise, pray for the salvation of our souls.* (Troparion to St. Xenia)

Bad Relationships

 THIS 13TH-CENTURY TUSCAN eloped at 17 with a nobleman, gave birth to a son, and lived as the nobleman's mistress for nine years. After he was murdered, she saw it as a sign and confessed to the affair. She returned to her father's house, but he would not accept her. She and her son were sheltered by the Franciscans at Cortona. Young and attractive, Margaret often fell back into bad relationships, followed by periods of self-loathing. She began caring for the sick and poor, and eventually founded a lay Franciscan group called the *Poverelle* (Poor Ones).

. . . .

RITUAL | PRAY THAT YOUR RELATIONSHIPS LEAD YOU TO THE JOY THAT GOD DESIRES FOR YOU.

. . . .

PRAYER | *Lord, teach me which desires will bring me happiness.*

MARGARET OF CORTONA

JOHN BOSCO

Unruly Children

 GIOVANNI MELCHIOR BOSCO was the son of Venerable Margaret Bosco and Francis Bosco, and was born in the Italian region of Piedmont in 1815. As a boy he imitated magicians to entertain other children, and would then repeat the homily he had heard in church. He had vivid dreams of trying to lead a crowd of unruly boys, which he later understood to be a sign of the work that God was calling him to undertake. He did many odd jobs before going to college and the seminary; after being ordained in 1841 he began to teach. Later in his life Pius IX asked him to write down his dreams as a gift to his followers, the Salesians. To this day the Salesians' primary ministry is to young people.

....

RITUAL | WRITE DOWN YOUR DREAMS AND BRING THEM INTO PRAYER, ASKING GOD TO SHOW YOU HOW THEY MIGHT HELP YOU IMAGINE THE GREATER LIFE TO WHICH GOD IS INVITING YOU.

....

PRAYER | *God, show me how I might use my gifts. Help me as you helped John Bosco to see how I might serve people and help build your kingdom.*

Sick Children

 BORN IN THE MID-7TH CENTURY, Pharaildis had by the 12th century achieved renown in Ghent, such that a church and an order of canons were named after her. The sister of St. Gudule and niece of St. Gertrude of Nivelle, she was married against her will and never consummated her marriage, often staying in churches late into the night. By the mid-8th century her relics were venerated and were brought to Ghent by the abbot of a monastery there. Her patronage of sick children arose from a legend that described a spring that cured them.

. . . .

RITUAL | BLESS A SICK CHILD BY USING HOLY WATER TO TRACE THE CROSS ON THEIR FOREHEAD.

. . . .

PRAYER | *Lord, bless this child with health.*

PHARAILDIS

ALOYSIUS GONZAGA

Pandemics

 ALOYSIUS WAS a 16th-century noble from a well-known family. He was destined to inherit the title of marquis, but after travels to Spain decided to join the newly formed Society of Jesus and did so in 1585, against his family's wishes. During his early studies in Rome he regularly went out to serve the victims of the plague there, and died at 23 years of age. His spiritual adviser, St. Robert Bellarmine, asked at his own death to be buried with St. Aloysius.

....

RITUAL | BE GENEROUS WITH YOUR TIME WITH A SICK PERSON. HOLD THAT PERSON'S HAND OR RUB THEIR BACK. FIND SOME WAY TO SHOW YOU ARE NOT AFRAID OF THEIR BODY.

....

PRAYER | *Lord, I pray that my fear of disease may not keep me from loving those who are sick. May I praise you in both health and sickness.*

Pregnancy

THE MOTHER OF THE VIRGIN MARY, Anne's name was Hannah in Hebrew, and she had much in common with Hannah, the mother of the prophet Samuel. Both were childless; both begged God for a child; and both were granted children who were destined to be great. Anne was venerated in Eastern churches for centuries, and after the publication in the 13th century of Jacob of Voragine's renowned book, *The Golden Legend*, she became well known in Western churches.

RITUAL | DURING PREGNANCY, BEGIN EACH DAY BY BLESSING YOUR CHILD, BY PLACING YOUR HANDS UPON YOUR GROWING WOMB AND PRAYING THE WORDS OF HANNAH.

PRAYER |

> *My heart exults in the Lord, my horn is exalted in my God. There is no Holy One like the Lord; there is no Rock like our God.*
> (From the prayer of Hannah, 1 Samuel 2:1)

Addictions

 THIS CONVENTUAL FRANCISCAN founded monasteries, established Catholic newspapers in Poland and Japan, earned a Doctor of Theology degree, and taught at a seminary. During the rise of the Third Reich, his monastery of Niepokalanow in Teresin, outside Warsaw sheltered some 3,000 people, mostly Jewish, from the Nazis. He was captured and sent to Auschwitz as prisoner number 16670. Maximilian knew the desolation of loss of freedom, and having sacrificed himself to save another prisoner, reminds us that true freedom is won only in the risk of love.

....

PRAYER | *St. Maximilian, even in prison you were free. Help me to grow in the freedom to love as generously as you did in your life. Pray for those who are losing their freedom to addiction, that they too might have hope.*

MAXIMILIAN KOLBE

Hospitals, Nurses, the Sick

 João was born in Portugal, but moved to Spain at an early age and worked as a shepherd. He also fought in Africa under Charles V and as a mercenary. He had a conversion experience in his forties in which Jesus called him "John of God." As a result he left the military and returned to Spain to serve the sick, poor, and homeless of Granada. For a time he was sent to a hospital for the insane. He was the spiritual student of St. John of Ávila. He later founded the Order of Hospitalers of St. John of God.

....

RITUAL | PRAY FOR THOSE IN THE HOSPITAL EVERY TIME YOU PASS BY ONE.

....

PRAYER | *Lord, may the sick praise you in their sickness, and may you bless them with gifts of healing.*

JOHN OF GOD

MARGARET OF CASTELLO

Disability

 MARGARET WAS BORN in 1287, blind, hunchbacked, and a dwarf, with one leg shorter than the other. Her father put her in a cell next to the parish church when she was just six. At 17, her parents abandoned her and she became a beggar. Other beggars befriended her and she was eventually given a home by some families of means. She became a Dominican tertiary and was loved by many. People thronged to her funeral in Città di Castello in Umbria, because she was known as a bringer of peace. When a disabled girl was cured during the funeral, the parish priest allowed Margaret's body to be interred under the altar, where it remains today.

....

RITUAL | LEARN ABOUT THE FAITH-BASED L'ARCHE COMMUNITY, OR SOME SIMILAR HOME FOR THE DISABLED.

....

PRAYER | *O God, by whose will the blessed virgin Margaret was blind from birth—that the eyes of her mind being inwardly enlightened, she might think without ceasing on you alone—be the light of our eyes, that we may be able to flee the shadows of this world and reach the home of never-ending light. We ask this through Christ, our Lord.* (From the General Calendar of the Order of Preachers)

Healthy Throats

 THE FEAST DAY OF BLAISE, February 3, is still a popular celebration among many Catholics today. The blessing of throats recalls a story about this 2nd–3rd-century physician and bishop, who once saved a child from choking on a fish bone.

....

RITUAL | VISIT A CHURCH ON FEBRUARY 3 FOR A THROAT BLESSING.

....

PRAYER | *O God, deliver us through the intercession of your holy bishop and martyr Blaise from all evil of soul and body, especially from all ills of the throat; and grant us the grace to make a good confession in the confident hope of obtaining your pardon, and ever to praise with worthy lips your most holy name. Through Christ our Lord. Amen.* (From the Novena in Honor of St. Blaise)

BLAISE

SEBASTIAN

Injuries

 IN THE 4TH CENTURY St. Ambrose wrote a biography of his fellow Milanese, Sebastian, who had died a century earlier. Sebastian had been a captain of the Praetorian Guard under Diocletian, and had converted a number of people. Upon learning that Sebastian was a Christian, the emperor ordered him to be shot with arrows. Sebastian survived and returned to preach, but Diocletian then had him beaten to death. In the 14th century the spread of the plague was likened to being shot by arrows, and Sebastian was called upon as an intercessor.

. . . .

RITUAL | WHEN YOU ARE INJURED, THANK GOD FOR THE REMINDER OF THE PASSING NATURE OF LIFE IN THE FLESH.

. . . .

PRAYER | *Lord, help us devote all our bodily strength to coming to know you and witness you.*

Mental Illness

 PELAGIA IVANOVNA SEMBRENIKOVA, a yurodivyi, or "fool for Christ," is often called Pelagia the Holy Fool. She was born in the early 19th century in Arzamas, near Moscow. As a young married woman she went to St. Seraphim of Sarov, who gave her a mission to defend orphans. On returning home she began acting as though mad. Her husband locked her up and eventually abandoned her. After four years spent homeless, Pelagia was approached by Anna, a holy nun, who persuaded her to move to the convent at Diveyevo, where she lived for the rest of her life. Anna cared for her, while the other nuns misunderstood her and considered her crazy. However, Pelagia showed great spiritual gifts, probing hearts and minds and performing cures.

....

RITUAL | DO SOMETHING OUTLANDISH OUT OF LOVE.

....

PRAYER | *We are fools on Christ's account, but you are wise in Christ; we are weak, but you are strong; you are held in honor, but we in disrepute. To this very hour we go hungry and thirsty, we are poorly clad and roughly treated, we wander about homeless and we toil, working with our own hands.* (1 Corinthians 4:10–12)

PELAGIA IVANOVNA

RAPHAEL

Recovery from Illness

 ONE OF THREE ANGELS named in the biblical texts, Raphael (meaning "God heals") figures prominently in the deuterocanonical *Book of Tobit* as the angel who guards the main character, Tobias, and heals a blind man.

RITUAL | AFTER RECOVERY FROM ILLNESS, PRAY A NOVENA (A PRAYER OVER NINE DAYS) IN THANKSGIVING FOR HEALTH, AND IN PETITION FOR THOSE WHO ARE STILL SICK, USING THE WORDS GIVEN BELOW.

PRAYER | *Angel, guide of Tobias, lay the request we now address to you at the feet of Him on whose unveiled Face you are privileged to gaze. Lonely and tired, crushed by the separations and sorrows of life, we feel the need of calling you and of pleading for the protection of your wings, so that we may not be as strangers in the province of joy, all ignorant of the concerns of our country. Remember the weak, you who are strong, you whose home lies beyond the region of thunder, in a land that is always peaceful, always serene and bright with the resplendent glory of God.* (From a Prayer to St. Raphael)

Emotional & Nervous Disorders

 TORN WITH GRIEF at the loss of his wife, the 6th–7th-century Celtic king Damon lost his mind and made advances on his daughter Dymphna. When he found her in Geel in Belgium, he killed her. Over the centuries healings were attributed to her, and many people with emotional disorders made a pilgrimage to her tomb in Geel. By the 15th century canons of the church instructed local families to take in the overflow of patient-pilgrims, beginning the custom of integrating them into the life of the community, which continues to this day.

....

RITUAL | TREAT THOSE WHO SUFFER FROM EMOTIONAL AND NERVOUS DISORDERS WITH CARE; TRY TO HELP THEM TO FEEL PART OF THE COMMUNITY.

....

PRAYER | *Lord, grant hope to those who suffer from nervous disorders; free them from their burden.*

DYMPHNA

THOMAS AQUINAS

Happiness

 THE "ANGELIC DOCTOR" was born in 1225 to the Italian Count of Aquino. He studied under Albert the Great in Paris, where he later taught and wrote copiously, culminating in his *Summa Theologica*, a significant theological work in the West to this day. In it, he describes happiness as the vision of God, the fulfillment of all human desire. Thomas abandoned the work after a revelation that made him consider his writing as a straw in the wind compared to the glory of God.

. . . .

RITUAL | SING THOMAS'S FAMOUS PRAYER *PANGE LINGUA* ON HOLY THURSDAY.

. . . .

PRAYER | *Down in adoration falling,*
Lo! the sacred Host we hail,
Lo! o'er ancient forms departing
Newer rites of grace prevail;
Faith for all defects supplying,
Where the feeble senses fail.
To the everlasting Father,
And the Son Who reigns on high
With the Holy Ghost proceeding
Forth from Each eternally,
Be salvation, honor, blessing,
Might and endless majesty.
(Thomas Aquinas, from Pange Lingua, translated by Edward Caswall, 1873)

THOMAS THE APOSTLE

Doubt

THE MOST WELL-KNOWN description of Thomas the apostle comes in Chapter 20 of the Gospel of John. The other disciples are present when the risen Jesus appears to them. When they recount the story to Thomas, he will not believe until he can touch the wounds in Jesus' body. Eight days later he has that opportunity; Jesus' reply to him is that Thomas is blessed by seeing, but "blessed are they that have not seen, but believe," aptly describing Jesus' later followers.

. . . .

RITUAL | SINCE DOUBT IS A SHADOW THAT ACCOMPANIES THE LIFE OF FAITH, IMAGINE YOURSELF IN THOMAS' SHOES. PUT YOURSELF IN THE STORY AND VISUALIZE HOW YOU MIGHT REACT IN A SIMILAR POSITION.

. . . .

PRAYER | *Lord, I believe. Help my unbelief!* (Compare Mark 9:24)

Depression

 TIKHON WAS BORN in 1724 to a destitute family in the Novgorod region of Russia. He was named Bishop of Voronezh in 1763 and served there for seven years before retiring to the monastery of Zadonsk, where he lived for the rest of his life. He struggled with depression for much of his adult years.

....

PRAYER | *You have been an example for all by word, life, love, faith, purity, and humility. Therefore, you now abide in the heavenly mansions, where you stand before the throne of the All-holy Trinity. Holy Hierarch Tikhon, pray for the salvation of our souls.* (St. Tikhon of Zadonsk, Troparion, Tone 8)

....

TIKHON OF ZADONSK

GENEVIÈVE

Disasters

 THE PATRONESS OF PARIS was a 5th-century girl who met St. Germanus of Auxerre and expressed her desire for a religious life. She professed at the age of 15, and was renowned for her piety. In time the bishop of the city appointed her to oversee the religious communities of women. Their prayers helped the city avoid the sack of Attila the Hun, and later other armies. Over the centuries, processions and reverence of Geneviève's relics helped the city to avoid natural disasters.

· ·

RITUAL | DONATE TO A DISASTER RELIEF CHARITY.

· ·

PRAYER | *Give us, Lord, the spirit of intelligence and love of which you filled your daughter, Geneviève, so that, attentive to your service and seeking to do your will, we can please you by our faith and our deeds.* (Litany to St. Geneviève)

Fear

 JEANNE D'ARC was born in 1412 in Donrémy, France. At the age of 13, she heard the voices of St. Michael, St. Catherine of Alexandria, and St. Margaret of Antioch, exhorting her to help the Dauphin overcome English rule of France. Three years later, Joan went to Charles VII; subsequently she led troops into battle, earned several victories between 1429 and 1430, and brought Charles VII to the throne. The Burgundians captured Joan and sold her to the English, who tried and executed her as a heretic. Later Pope Callixtus III reviewed the case and declared her a martyr.

JOAN OF ARC

....

RITUAL | WHEN YOU ARE AFRAID, CALL UPON ST. JOAN AND ASK FOR HER PRAYERS.

....

PRAYER | *Joan, you were afraid when God called you to a task you thought impossible. Pray for us in our fear, that we too might move forward in the confidence that God will strengthen us for all good work.*

JUDE

Hopelessness

 ONE OF THE TWELVE original disciples of Jesus, Jude went to preach in Mesopotamia, Syria, and Persia. For centuries he was identified as the author of the New Testament Epistle of Jude, though recent biblical criticism calls that into question. Devotion to this saint, and his association with hopeless causes, probably arises from themes in that letter, but may also be related to the similarity between his name and that of Judas Iscariot, who betrayed Jesus.

....

RITUAL | PRAY ABOUT A PARTICULARLY DIFFICULT SITUATION USING A ST. JUDE NOVENA.

....

PRAYER | *St. Jude, faithful servant and friend of Jesus, the Church honors and invokes you universally, as the patron of hopeless cases, of things almost despaired of. Pray for me, I am so helpless and alone. Make use, I implore you, of that particular privilege given to you, to bring visible and speedy help where help is almost despaired of.* (Novena to St. Jude)

Anger

BORN AROUND 342 as Eusebius
Hieronymous Sophronius, Jerome is
best known as the translator of the
Latin Bible known as the Vulgate. One of the
doctors of the Church, he wrote voluminously
on the scriptures, theology, and history. In his
letters he betrayed his well-known tendencies
toward anger and vindictiveness, earning him
a number of enemies and friends. He worked
to manage his temper through asceticism and
study, living for his last 34 years in the Holy
Land as a hermit.

JEROME

....

RITUAL | WHEN YOU STRUGGLE WITH ANGER,
FOLLOW JEROME'S EXAMPLE OF STUDYING
THE SCRIPTURES IN ORDER TO KNOW CHRIST
MORE FULLY.

....

PRAYER | *Lord, you who know me better than
I know myself, help me to see other people as
other Christs.*

JEANNE DE CHANTAL

Debt

 BORN A NOBLE in 1572, Jeanne Frances Fremiot married the Baron of Chantal and thereby inherited a pile of debt. She managed to bring the household under control through austere living. At 28 she was widowed with four children and was forced to live in the house of her father-in-law for seven years. She met Francis de Sales, who became her spiritual director. After providing for her children, she founded the Congregation of the Visitation of Our Lady in 1610. The order was designed for widows and lay women; eventually 69 convents were founded.

....

RITUAL | IDENTIFY THE GREAT GOOD TO WHICH THE LORD IS CALLING YOU, AND ALWAYS MAKE FINANCIAL DECISIONS WITH THAT IN MIND.

....

PRAYER | *Lord, you helped Jeanne restore order to her house; help me restore order to mine.*

Consolation & Desolation

 AFTER A PROFOUND CONVERSION experience in 1522, young Spanish soldier Ignatius secluded himself in a cave to discern God's will for his life, writing his book *Spiritual Exercises*. It is perhaps the most widely used guide for helping people understand the spiritual aspects of consolation and desolation, which point them toward understanding the purposes for which God has created their lives. Ignatius described a disordered will as a drop of water on a rock, but God's will as a drop of water on a sponge.

RITUAL | AT THE END OF EACH DAY, SPEND 10 MINUTES IN PRAYER ASKING THESE QUESTIONS: FOR WHAT AM I MOST THANKFUL? WHAT DOES GOD WANT ME TO PAY ATTENTION TO? IN WHAT EVENTS OF THE PAST DAY DO I SEE GOD AT WORK? WHAT DO I REGRET? WHAT GIVES ME HOPE?

PRAYER | *Take, Lord, and receive all my liberty, my memory, my understanding, my entire will— all I have and possess. You have given these to me; now I return them to you, to use according to your will. Give me only your love and your grace; these are enough for me.* (St. Ignatius Loyola)

IGNATIUS OF LOYOLA

JOHN VIANNEY

Listening

BY THE END of his life, nearly 75,000 people a year came to confess their sins to Jean Baptiste Marie Vianney, a French curé (parish priest). So great was his renown as a listener that he spent up to 16 hours a day in the confessional. Vianney was born in 1786 in Dardilly, France. He was assigned to the town of Ars, where he devoted himself to his parishioners. They described him as having a remarkable gift for understanding their souls, and his fame spread rapidly.

RITUAL | PRACTICE THE ART OF LISTENING NEXT TIME YOU ARE WITH SOMEONE YOU LOVE.

PRAYER | *I love you, O my God, and my sole desire is to love you until the last breath of my life. I love you, O infinitely lovable God, and I prefer to die loving you than live one instant without loving you.*
(Act of Love, Curé of Ars)

Forgiveness

 THE FIRST CHRISTIAN MARTYR (Greek for "witness"), Stephen, was one of seven deacons appointed by the disciples of Jesus. Luke describes him as "full of grace and power" in his preaching. His enemies accused him of blasphemy, bringing him before the court. He was condemned to death by stoning, but after seeing a vision of Jesus at the right hand of God, he echoed Jesus' own forgiveness of his enemies: "Lord, do not hold this sin against them."

....

PRAYER | *Grant to us, we beseech you, O Lord, so to imitate what we revere that we may learn to love even our enemies: for we celebrate him who could even plead on behalf of his persecutors with your Son Our Lord Jesus Christ.* (From a St. Stephen litany)

....

STEPHEN

MARY, MOTHER OF SORROWS

Sorrow

 In Luke's gospel, Simeon tells the mother of Jesus that her soul will be pierced because of what her son will mean for Israel. At Jesus' crucifixion it is clear what he meant: she will suffer greatly to see her innocent son killed. Mary is the mother of sorrows, even as she is the mother of God's great blessing to the world.

....

RITUAL | PRAY THE SORROWFUL MYSTERIES OF THE ROSARY (THE AGONY IN THE GARDEN; THE WHIPPING AT THE PILLAR; THE CROWNING WITH THORNS; THE WAY OF THE CROSS; AND THE CRUCIFIXION). FOR EACH MYSTERY, PRAY ONE "OUR FATHER" FOLLOWED BY TEN "HAIL MARYS" AND THE "GLORY BE."

....

PRAYER | *Hail, Holy Queen, mother of mercy, our life, our sweetness, and our hope. To you do we cry, poor banished children of Eve; to you do we cry, mourning and weeping in this valley of tears. Turn then, most gracious advocate, your eyes of mercy toward us, and show us unto the blessed fruit of your womb, Jesus. O clement, O loving, O sweet Virgin Mary. Pray for us, O holy mother of God, that we may be worthy of the promises of Christ.* (Salve Regina)

NORBERT OF XANTEN

Peacemaking

NORBERT WAS BORN around 1080 in the German town of Xanten, and was later ordained to the subdiaconate. He was a clerical opportunist, but experienced a conversion and decided to dedicate himself to ministry as a parish priest. Seeking to reform lax practices, he became a wandering preacher, encountering the violence of armed knights and the cynicism of clergy and peasants. Influenced by the reforms of the Cistercian monks, he sought to bring peace by reforms among servant-minded priests. He founded an order at Prémontré in France, and was later named Archbishop of Madgeburg.

．．

RITUAL | BRING PEACE TO THE WORLD FIRST BY GROWING IN HOLINESS: LEARN PRAYER.

．．

PRAYER | *Lord, make me an instrument of your peace.* (From the prayer of St. Francis)

Hope

 A Spanish Carmelite mystic and later doctor of the Church, Teresa was born Teresa Sánchez de Cepeda y Ahumada in 1515. Her nobleman father frowned upon her desire for religious life, but she entered the convent secretly at 20, battling illness even as she experienced visions. Concerned that the visions might be diabolical, she received direction from the Jesuit (St.) Francis Borgia, who helped persuade her that they were from God. At the heart of her mystical theology was a great hope of the soul's union with the beloved: "Contemplative prayer in my opinion is nothing else than a close sharing between friends; it means taking time frequently to be alone with him who we know loves us." (From The Book of Her Life, 8:5)

RITUAL | PRAY SILENTLY EVERY DAY AND WAIT UPON THE GOD WHO LOVES YOU.

PRAYER | *Hope, O my soul, hope. You know neither the day nor the hour. Watch carefully, for everything passes quickly, even though your impatience makes doubtful what is certain, and turns a very short time into a long one.* (St. Teresa of Ávila, Exclamaciones 15:3)

TERESA OF ÁVILA

JANUARY

1	ZEDISLAVA BERKA
2	BASIL THE GREAT, GREGORY OF NAZIANZEN
3	GENEVIÈVE
4	PHARAILDIS, ELIZABETH ANN SETON
5	JOHN NEPOMUCENE NEUMANN
6	MELCHIOR, CASPAR, BALTHASAR
7	RAYMOND OF PEÑAFORT
8	ANGELA OF FOLIGNO
9	ADRIAN OF CANTERBURY
10	GREGORY OF NYSSA
11	THEODOSIUS
12	AELRED OF RIEVAULX
13	HILARY
14	FELIX OF NOLA
15	ITA OF KILLEEDY
16	BERARD & COMPANIONS
17	ANTHONY OF EGYPT
18	PRISCA
19	JOSEPH SEBASTIAN PELCZAR
20	SEBASTIAN
21	MAXIMOS THE CONFESSOR
22	VINCENT & ANASTASIUS
23	TIMOTHY
24	FRANCIS DE SALES
25	DWYNWEN
26	TIMOTHY & TITUS
27	ANGELA MERICI
28	THOMAS AQUINAS
29	GILDAS
30	PELAGIA IVANOVNA
31	JOHN BOSCO

St. Francis de Sales

St. John Bosco

1   PETER HONG PYONG-JU &
     PAUL HONG YONG-JU

2   ALFRED DELP

3   BLAISE

4   RABANUS MAURUS

5   AGATHA

6   KSENYA BLAZHENNAYA,
     JAPANESE MARTYRS

7   COLETTE

8   JOSEPHINE BAKHITA

9   MIGUEL FEBRES CORDERO

10   SCHOLASTICA

11   SEVERINUS

12   JULIAN THE HOSPITALLER

13   CATHERINE DE'RICCI

14   VALENTINE

15   CLAUDE DE LA COLOMBIÈRE

16   GILBERT OF SEMPRINGHAM

17   SEVEN FOUNDERS OF THE
      ORDER OF SERVITES

18   FRA ANGELICO

19   CONRAD OF PIACENZA

20   BLESSED JACINTA &
      FRANCISCO MARTO

21   PETER DAMIAN

22   MARGARET OF CORTONA

23   POLYCARP

24   CARTHAGINIAN MARTYRS

25   WALBURGA

26   PORPHYRY OF GAZA

27   MARIA CARIDAD BRADER

28   OSWALD OF WORCESTER

29   JOHN CASSIAN

FEBRUARY

St. Josephine Bakhita

St. Fra Angelico

MARCH

1	DAVID OF WALES
2	MARTYRS UNDER ALEXANDER
3	KATHARINE DREXEL
4	CASIMIR
5	JOHN JOSEPH OF THE CROSS
6	SYLVESTER OF ASSISI
7	PERPETUA & FELICITY
8	JOHN OF GOD
9	CATHERINE OF BOLOGNA
10	JOHN OGILVIE
11	EULOGIUS OF CÓRDOBA
12	JOSEPH TSANG-TA-PONG
13	NICEPHORUS OF CONSTANTINOPLE
14	MATILDA
15	LOUISE DE MARILLAC
16	CLEMENT MARY HOFBAUER
17	PATRICK
18	CYRIL OF JERUSALEM
19	JOSEPH
20	CUTHBERT
21	NICHOLAS OF FLÜE
22	NICHOLAS OWEN
23	TURIBIUS OF MONGROVEJO
24	CATHERINE OF SWEDEN
25	DISMAS
26	LUDGER OF MÜNSTER
27	RUPERT
28	HESYCHIUS OF JERUSALEM
29	JONAS & BARACHISIUS
30	JOHN CLIMACUS
31	STEPHEN OF MAR SABA

St. Catherine of Bologna

St. Patrick

APRIL

St. Giuseppe Moscati

St. Gianna Beretta Molla

MAY

St. Bernard of Montjoux

St. Joan of Arc

1   PEREGRINE LAZIOSI
2   ATHANASIUS
3   PHILIP & JAMES THE LESS
4   JEAN-MARTIN MOYË
5   IRENE OF THESSALONICA
6   COLMAN MAC UI CLUASIGH
7   JOHN OF BEVERLEY
8   JULIAN OF NORWICH
9   PACHOMIUS
10 DAMIEN OF MOLOKAI
11 MATTEO RICCI
12 PANCRAS
13 ANDREW FOURNET
14 MATTHIAS THE APOSTLE
15 DYMPHNA, ISIDORE THE FARMER
16 BRENDAN THE NAVIGATOR
17 PASCAL BAYLON
18 POPE JOHN I
19 DUNSTAN OF CANTERBURY
20 BERNARDINO OF SIENA
21 EUGENE DE MAZENOD
22 RITA OF CASCIA
23 WILLIAM OF ROCHESTER
24 SYMEON STYLITES THE YOUNGER
25 MEXICAN MARTYRS
26 PHILIP NERI
27 AUGUSTINE OF CANTERBURY
28 BERNARD OF MONTJOUX
29 MAXIMINUS OF TRIER
30 JOAN OF ARC
31 NICOLAS BARRÉ

JUNE

1	JUSTIN MARTYR
2	ERASMUS OF FORMIA
3	UGANDAN MARTYRS
4	FILIPPO SMALDONE
5	FRANCISCAN MARTYRS OF CHINA
6	NORBERT OF XANTEN
7	MARTYRS OF CÓRDOBA
8	WILLIAM OF YORK
9	COLUMBKILLE
10	BRIGID OF KILDARE
11	IGNAZIO CHOUKRALLAH MALOYAN
12	POLISH MARTYRS OF THE NAZIS
13	ANTHONY OF PADUA
14	DOGMAEL OF WALES
15	GERMAIN COUSIN
16	CURIG OF WALES
17	BOTOLPH OF IKANHOE
18	ELIZABETH OF SCHÖNAU
19	JULIANA FALCONIERI
20	IRISH MARTYRS
21	ALOYSIUS GONZAGA
22	THOMAS MORE
23	BASIL HOPKO
24	ROMAN MARTYRS UNDER NERO
25	CYNEBURGA OF GLOUCESTER
26	ANDREA GIACINTO LONGHIN
27	CYRIL OF ALEXANDRIA
28	IRENAEUS OF LYONS
29	PAUL & PETER
30	VINCENT YEN

St. Anthony of Padua

St. Paul

JULY

1 OLIVER PLUNKETT

2 SWITHUN

3 THOMAS THE APOSTLE

4 ELIZABETH OF PORTUGAL

5 ANTHONY MARY ZACCARIA

6 MARIA GORETTI

7 PETER TO ROT

8 PRISCILLA & AQUILA

9 AUGUSTINE ZHAO RONG
& COMPANIONS

10 THEODOSIUS PECHERSKY

11 BENEDICT OF NURSIA

12 VERONICA

13 TERESA OF THE ANDES

14 CAMILLUS OF LELLIS,
KATERI TEKAKWITHA

15 BONAVENTURE

16 MARTYRS OF BRAZIL

17 CARMELITE MARTYRS OF
COMPIÈGNE

18 THENEVA

19 MACRINA THE YOUNGER

20 MARGARET OF ANTIOCH

21 FRANCIS DE MONTMORENCY LAVAL

22 MARY MAGDALENE

23 BRIDGET OF SWEDEN

24 CHRISTINA THE ASTONISHING

25 CHRISTOPHER

26 ANNE & JOACHIM

27 CUNEGUNDES

28 PEDRO POVEDA CASTROVERDE

29 MARTHA

30 PETER CHRYSOLOGUS

31 SOLANUS CASEY,
IGNATIUS OF LOYOLA

St. Thomas the Apostle

St. Anne

AUGUST

1	ALPHONSUS MARIA OF LIGUORI
2	PETER JULIAN EYMUND
3	GAMALIEL
4	JOHN VIANNEY
5	NONNA
6	MARIA FRANCESCA RUBATTO
7	CAJETAN
8	MARY MACKILLOP
9	EDITH STEIN
10	LAWRENCE OF ROME
11	JOHN HENRY NEWMAN
12	CLARE OF ASSISI
13	TIKHON OF ZADONSK
14	MAXIMILIAN KOLBE
15	ISIDORE BAKANJA
16	ROCH
17	JEANNE OF THE CROSS DELANOUE
18	HELENA
19	JOHN EUDES
20	BERNARD OF CLAIRVAUX
21	VICTOIRE RASOAMANARIVO
22	JOHN KEMBLE
23	ROSE OF LIMA
24	BARTHOLOMEW THE APOSTLE
25	LOUIS IX
26	TERESA DE GESU JORNET Y IBARS
27	MONICA
28	LOUIS & ZÉLIE MARTIN, AUGUSTINE
29	JOHN THE BAPTIST
30	PAMMACHIUS
31	AIDAN OF LINDISFARNE

St. Alphonsus Maria of Liguori

St. Maximilian Kolbe

121

SEPTEMBER

St. Frédéric Ozanam

St. Joseph of Cupertino

1 GILES

2 MARTYRS OF SEPTEMBER

3 GREGORY THE GREAT

4 IDA OF HERZFELD

5 TERESA OF CALCUTTA

6 THOMAS TSUJI

7 IGNATIUS KLOPOTOWSKI

8 CORBINIAN

9 FRÉDÉRIC OZANAM

10 NICHOLAS OF TOLENTINO

11 CHARLES SPINOLA

12 GUY OF ANDERLECHT

13 JOHN CHRYSOSTOM

14 GABRIEL JOHN TAUIN DU-FRESSE

15 MARY, MOTHER OF SORROWS

16 CYPRIAN OF CARTHAGE

17 HILDEGARD OF BINGEN

18 JOSEPH OF CUPERTINO

19 EMILY DE RODAT

20 KOREAN MARTYRS

21 MATTHEW THE APOSTLE

22 MARTYRS OF VALENCIA

23 PADRE PIO

24 ANTON MARTIN SLOMSEK

25 SERGIUS

26 COSMAS AND DAMIAN

27 VINCENT DE PAUL

28 BERNARDINO OF FELTRE

29 RAPHAEL & GABRIEL
    THE ARCHANGELS

30 JEROME

OCTOBER

1	THÉRÈSE OF LISIEUX
2	JAN BEYZYM
3	MOTHER THEODORE GUÉRIN
4	FRANCIS OF ASSISI
5	FAUSTINA KOWALSKA
6	BARTOLO LONGO
7	DUBTHACH
8	PELAGIA THE PENITENT
9	DIONYSIUS THE AREOPAGITE
10	FRANCIS BORGIA
11	JOHN XXIII
12	WILFRID OF YORK
13	EDWARD THE CONFESSOR
14	MARIE POUSSEPIN
15	TERESA OF ÁVILA
16	MARGUERITE D'YOUVILLE
17	IGNATIUS OF ANTIOCH
18	LUKE THE EVANGELIST
19	NORTH AMERICAN MARTYRS
20	BERTILLA BOSCARDIN
21	LAURA MONTOYA Y UPEGUI
22	DONATUS OF FIESOLE
23	BOETHIUS
24	ANTHONY MARY CLARET
25	FORTY MARTYRS OF ENGLAND & WALES
26	ALFRED THE GREAT
27	EMILINA
28	JUDE
29	GAETANO ERRICO
30	DOROTHY OF MONTAU
31	FOILLAN

St. Francis of Assisi

St. Teresa of Ávila

NOVEMBER

St. Martin de Porres

St. Albert the Great

1	ALL SAINTS
2	ALL SOULS
3	HUBERT OF LIÈGE AND MARTÍN DE PORRES
4	CHARLES BORROMEO
5	ELIZABETH
6	ILLTYD
7	JOHN DUNS SCOTUS
8	ELIZABETH OF THE TRINITY
9	MARÍA DEL CARMEN OF THE CHILD JESUS
10	LEO THE GREAT
11	MARTIN OF TOURS
12	JOSAPHAT
13	HOMOBONUS
14	LAWRENCE O'TOOLE
15	ALBERT THE GREAT
16	GERTRUDE THE GREAT
17	GREGORY THAUMATURGUS
18	ROSE PHILIPPINE DUCHESNE
19	ELIZABETH OF HUNGARY
20	MARIA FORTUNATA VITI
21	ALBERT OF LOUVAIN
22	MARTYRS OF ARMENIA
23	MIGUEL PRO
24	VIETNAMESE MARTYRS
25	LUIGI BELTRAME QUATTROCCHI
26	GAETANA STERNI
27	FRANCESCO ANTONIO FASANI
28	CATHERINE LABOURÉ
29	REDEMPTORUS OF THE CROSS
30	ANDREW THE APOSTLE

DECEMBER

1 CHARLES DE FOUCAULD
2 LIDUINA MENEGUZZI
3 FRANCIS XAVIER
4 CLEMENT OF ALEXANDRIA
5 PHILIP RINALDI
6 NICHOLAS OF MYRA
7 AMBROSE OF MILAN
8 ROMARIC
9 JUAN DIEGO CUAUTLATOATZIN
10 EULALIA
11 MARÍA MARAVILLAS DE JESÚS
12 JEANNE DE CHANTAL
13 LUCY
14 JOHN OF THE CROSS
15 MARY FRANCES SCHERVIER
16 MARY FONTANELLA
17 JOSÉ MANYANET Y VIVES
18 FLANNAN OF KILLALOE
19 AUGUSTINE MOI VAN NGUYEN
20 DOMINIC OF SILOS
21 PETER CANISIUS
22 FRANCES XAVIER CABRINI
23 JOHN CANTIUS
24 MOCHUA OF TIMAHOE
25 JACOPONE DA TODI
26 STEPHEN
27 JOHN THE EVANGELIST
28 THE HOLY INNOCENTS
29 THOMAS BECKET
30 MARGARET COLONNA
31 ZOTICUS OF CONSTANTINOPLE

St. Gaetana Sterni (November)

St. Francis Xavier

Index of Saints by Name

Index of Saints by Occasion

Further Reading

Butler, Alban. *Lives of the Saints* (various editions).

de Voragine, Jacobus. *The Golden Legend* (various English versions; some excerpts can be found online).

Farmer, David Hugh. *Oxford Dictionary of the Saints* (Oxford University Press, 2004).

Holböck, Ferdinand. *Married Saints and Blesseds through the Centuries* (Ignatius Press, 2002).

Web Site Information

DOWNLOADING SAINTS FOR YOUR COMPUTER

To download saint images to use as your computer's desktop background, go to www.desktopsaints.com (the username is **desktopsaints**, and the password is **saints4reasons**). You will find all of the saints in this book grouped by chapter. The saints are ordered in each chapter on the Web site to match the book.

To make one of the saints your computer's desktop background, choose the appropriate chapter on the Web site, then scroll down and click on the computer icon beneath the picture of the saint you wish to use. You will be presented with a number of resolution options. To find out the correct resolution for your monitor, go to the Control Panel of your PC, select Personalization and then Display Settings. If you are using a Mac, load the System Preferences panel and click on Displays. Select the correct resolution; the saint image should then appear in the center of your screen.

If you are using Internet Explorer on a PC, right-click on the image and choose "Set as Background." If you are using Safari on a Mac, hold down the Control button, click on the image, and select "Use Image as Desktop Picture." If you are using a different browser and/or operating system you may need to download the image and manually set it to be your background.

DOWNLOADING SAINTS FOR YOUR CELL PHONE

To download a wallpaper for your cell phone, follow the instructions above, but click on the phone icon instead of the computer icon. Your cell phone's manual should detail the screen resolution that you need. To download the image, right-click on the image if you are using a PC, or hold the Control button and click on the image if you are using a Mac, then save the image to your computer. Your phone's manual should detail how you should copy the image from your computer onto your phone and also how to set it to be your wallpaper.

You can also download saint images directly to your cell phone. To do this, go to www.desktopsaints.com/phone on your cell phone's Internet browser. The username is **desktopsaints**, and the password is **saints4reasons**). Choose the appropriate chapter and scroll down to your saint just as you would if you were downloading the saint to a computer. Click on the phone icon and select the resolution your phone uses. Once the image has downloaded, follow the on-screen instructions to set it as wallpaper or consult your phone's manual.